Friday Forward

Inspiration & Motivation
to End Your Week
Stronger Than It Started

ROBERT GLAZER

simple **truths**
▶ Small books. BIG IMPACT.

Copyright © 2020 by Robert Glazer and Kendall Marketing Group, LLC
Cover and internal design © 2020 by Sourcebooks
Cover design by Jackie Cummings/Sourcebooks

Sourcebooks, the colophon, and Simple Truths are registered trademarks of Sourcebooks.

This publication is designed to provide accurate and authoritative information in regard
to the subject matter covered. It is sold with the understanding that the publisher is
not engaged in rendering legal, accounting, or other professional service. If legal advice
or other expert assistance is required, the services of a competent professional person
should be sought.—*From a Declaration of Principles Jointly Adopted by a Committee
of the American Bar Association and a Committee of Publishers and Associations*

All brand names and product names used in this book are trademarks,
registered trademarks, or trade names of their respective holders. Sourcebooks
is not associated with any product or vendor in this book.

Published by Simple Truths, an imprint of Sourcebooks
P.O. Box 4410, Naperville, Illinois 60567-4410
(630) 961-3900
sourcebooks.com

Library of Congress Cataloging-in-Publication Data

Names: Glazer, Robert (CEO), author.
Title: Friday forward : inspiration & motivation to end your week even
    stronger than you started it / Robert Glazer.
Description: Naperville, Illinois : Simple Truths, an imprint of
    Sourcebooks, [2020]
Identifiers: LCCN 2020019161 (print) | LCCN 2020019162 (ebook) |
    |Subjects: LCSH: Motivation (Psychology) | Inspiration. | Self-actualization
    (Psychology)
Classification: LCC BF503 .G55 2020 (print) | LCC BF503 (ebook) | DDC
    153.8--dc23
LC record available at https://lccn.loc.gov/2020019161
LC ebook record available at https://lccn.loc.gov/2020019162

Printed and bound in the United States of America.
MA 10 9 8 7 6 5 4 3 2 1

For everyone in the Friday Forward community. Thank you for your support and for taking the time to elevate others.

For Chloe, Max, and Zach.
You each inspire me to be better every day.

Table of Contents

INTRODUCTION   VII

SPIRITUAL CAPACITY   **1**

Raising Values   5   Having Potential   22

Moment of Clarity   8   A Dad's Influence   25

Beautiful Day   11   Moon Shot   27

Wishing Happiness   14   Breaking Bad   30

Myth of Work-Life Balance   16   Purpose and Pain   32

Freedom to Fail   18   Carpe Diem   35

Man with a Plan   20

INTELLECTUAL CAPACITY   **39**

Myth of the Overnight Success   43   Power of Keystone Habits   61

Sharing Belief   45   Life Hack   63

Urgent vs. Important   47   Saying No   66

Early Riser   50   BS of Busy   69

Being Lucky   53   Goals and Standards   71

World Class   55   Being Excellent   74

Stop-Doing List   58

PHYSICAL CAPACITY 77

Clutch Performers	81	True Team Sacrifice	99
Trough and Peak	83	Two Hours	100
The Grind	86	Color War	102
Breaking Barriers	89	Good Sportsmanship	104
Character Coach	91	Tri It	106
Peloton Principle	94	Putting Yourself First	109
Environmental Effect	96		

EMOTIONAL CAPACITY 111

Energy Vampires	115	Random Act of Kindness	132
With Gratitude	118	Justifying Our Contradictions	134
Choice Words	120	What Really Matters	136
Love and Hate	123	Problem Solving	138
Rose, Thorn, and Bud	126	Embracing Relationships	140
Having Doubt	128	Bad Week	143
Four Benefits of Travel	130		

CONCLUSION: WHAT DID YOU NEED? 147

ACKNOWLEDGMENTS 151

ABOUT THE AUTHOR 153

Introduction

This all started with a simple change I wanted to introduce into my life: improving my morning routine.

On the heels of a transformational leadership training program, I resolved to get up earlier and dedicate some time to quiet thinking, writing, and reading something inspiring or positive to start my day.

This is not as easy a task as it should be in today's world. Many of us begin our mornings reactively and negatively, with crisis-driven news programming, social media apps vying for our attention, or a pile of emails about problems that occurred overnight. This type of morning can make it feel like the day is lost before it's even started.

The problem was, I hadn't found anything inspirational that really resonated with me. A lot of the quote books and other recommended readings in inspiration were a little too rainbow and unicorn-y for me.

However, I had a collection of stories and quotes I found inspiring in a different way that I had saved in an email folder.

So I decided to try an experiment and began sending a weekly email to the roughly forty people on my team at Acceleration Partners. After all, I'd learned the lessons of most entrepreneurs well: if you don't find what you want, you should start it yourself. I called it Friday Inspiration and focused on stories that were inspirational but also thought-provoking and challenging.

The stories had nothing to do with our business. Instead, my goal with each message was to write something that I would be inspired to read and that would push the team to improve across all facets of their lives. I figured that sending the messages each Friday morning was a good way to start the weekend on the right foot.

That was my primary goal. I didn't have a master plan or long-term vision of spreading these messages to a wider audience. Really, I expected the emails to be skimmed or even ignored each week. I did it anyway because I enjoyed the writing process, and it became an important part of my own routine.

To my surprise, after a few weeks, I started to get replies. Several employees told me they looked forward to the messages and had shared them with friends and family. Some had also used them as motivation to begin to make changes in their lives, whether that meant running a race, setting personal goals, or upping their game at work. It was at this point that I first thought the emails might have value for people beyond our company's walls.

Soon after, I attended an event for a group of entrepreneurs where we were sharing best practices.

I shared my Friday Inspiration concept with other business leaders at the event and told them I was getting very positive feedback from my team. I suggested they try something similar in their own organizations and added them to my email list so they could see what I was writing or forward my notes to their teams.

Several CEOs took me up on my offer and began sharing my weekly note with their companies. Within weeks, many of them told me they were receiving the same positive feedback from their employees. One CEO even started his own weekly message to his team that he still sends each week.

I began to wonder if other people might find the content valuable. I set up a basic email template, made it possible to sign up, changed the name to Friday Forward (because it was being forwarded regularly), and put a few hundred people I knew on the list. I prepared for replies such as "what is this?" or "take me off this list," but they never came. Instead, I got the similarly positive feedback I had received from my own team. A few months later, someone wrote a piece in *Inc.* magazine titled "This Is the Only Newsletter I Read," and a few thousand people signed up in a week. From there, it really started to take off.

Almost five years later, and to my amazement, every week, over two hundred thousand people read Friday Forward in over sixty countries around the world. More rewardingly, each week, I receive replies from readers thanking me for the positive impact it's made on their lives.

As Friday Forward's reach expanded, it made an increasingly significant impact on me. Writing the Friday Forward each week became a keystone habit—discovering and reflecting on inspiring stories allowed me to start each day on a positive note and gave me a growing responsibility to elevate others. As the Friday Forward readership grew, my motivation to improve as a writer and deliver the best possible content and value to the growing community of readers grew along with it.

The topics I choose each week are related to things I want to learn or get better at myself, so I am inherently invested in each post. I often tie the Friday Forward to a personal anecdote or current issue, making sure that the topic is accessible to the entire audience, no matter who or where they are at that moment. And each post typically ends with reflective questions that challenge readers to consider their own journey and choices.

I believe this format has resonated because Friday Forward motivates us to grow, and the topics are actionable. It's definitely not rainbows and unicorns; the topics encourage us to push outside our comfort zone and question the limits of what we can accomplish. Growth doesn't come without challenge. I believe change comes from challenge and connection.

This feels especially urgent now. The evidence is pretty clear that growth comes from being pushed into the area of discomfort where we challenge our assumptions and our self-imposed limitations.

Despite this, our world is increasingly constructed to prevent that push. An alarming number of children are growing up under the influence of "snowplow parenting," parents who believe their role is to remove or mitigate the obstacles their children encounter. They go through a school system that rewards conformity and getting things right the first time, which diminishes creativity. They graduate into a world defined by a social media echo chamber that feeds people things they are algorithmically expected to like and shows them the curated top 5 percent of everyone's lives. For many, each day feels more exhausting and unfulfilling than the last.

This is a cycle that we need to break. We have to productively challenge each other—to lift people up while also pushing them to be their best selves. The messages of Friday Forward are just one important step. I believe that most of us are living below our full potential, and we have so much more capacity to achieve the life we want. In doing so, we can help others to accomplish the same.

The Four Capacities

The goal with Friday Forward has always been to help people grow, but it was only after I had written these messages for a few years and began developing my first book, *Elevate*, that the exact themes took shape. As I dug into the concepts behind each post, I realized they largely fell into one of four elements of capacity building.

Capacity building is the method through which we seek, acquire, and develop the skills we need to perform at a higher level and unlock our innate potential. Capacity building is best understood when broken into four areas—spiritual, intellectual, physical, and emotional capacity.

Spiritual capacity requires us to evaluate who we are and what we want most from life and then align our daily lives to those principles. This starts with determining our core beliefs and values, which can be difficult for many as it involves deep introspection and self-assessment.

Building spiritual capacity is vital to a fulfilling life—if you don't have a destination in mind, you may waste a lot of time and energy running in the wrong or disparate directions. We must determine what we want most and align our daily lives to pursuing it.

Intellectual capacity is how we improve our ability to think, learn, plan, and execute with discipline. Developing our intellectual capacity often involves setting and achieving goals, developing good routines and habits, and learning continuously. Think of it as improving your operating system.

The greater your intellectual capacity, the more you will achieve with the same expenditure of energy or effort.

Physical capacity is our ability to improve our health, well-being, and physical performance. While our brains help guide us through life, it's our bodies that are asked to do the heavy lifting day in and day out. That's why it's so important to maintain our health and wellness, challenge ourselves, manage our stress, and get the proper amount of sleep. When your body is tired and sluggish or your brain is fatigued, it makes doing anything more difficult.

Building physical capacity goes beyond just diet and exercise—it also requires us to manage how we deal with stress and how we equip ourselves to face inevitable obstacles.

Emotional capacity relates to how we react to challenging situations and people as well as the quality of our relationships. Improving emotional capacity is difficult for most as it requires managing your feelings, evaluating the best and most challenging aspects of your personality, and accepting a certain amount of uncertainty and unpredictability from both people and circumstances.

People with high emotional capacity can generally cope with

challenges better and move on from setbacks quickly. They also have positive relationships with people who bring them energy and distance themselves from people who drain their energy.

My first book, *Elevate*, showed what capacity building is and how to begin embracing it in your own life. This book shares some of my favorite stories with real-life examples that can inspire you to make those changes.

How to Use This Book

First, I'd encourage you to use this book as part of a positive and intentional morning routine. Each Friday Forward is built around inspiring ideas and lessons you can reflect upon in your morning thoughts and journaling.

Second, I hope this book will inspire you to begin something similar for the people around you, whether that's your friends and family, your team at work, or a classroom of students. The biggest thing I've learned is that this type of inspiration can grow beyond what you'd ever expect, and your lessons and stories can help the people around you. By sharing with others or even starting a discussion around these concepts, you can lift others as you rise.

You might be thinking, "I've barely got my own life together. How am I supposed to do this for others?" Don't sell yourself short. All of us have the power to inspire at least one other person each day. Just try one simple thing today. Share an inspirational quote or a story that you find uplifting. My experience is the smallest gesture can make an enormous difference, especially if it hits someone at the right time.

Deep down, we're all hungry for inspiration, and you'd be surprised how quickly people will engage if they see you are genuinely looking to help them improve. We desperately need to stop spending so much time and energy knocking one another down and instead find ways to lift one another up. The former is a vicious cycle that lowers our moral compass while the latter is a virtuous one that raises the bar.

Don't get overwhelmed. Starting small is often the best way to begin creating lasting change and impact. That's the foundation of capacity building—making small, intentional changes that compound over time. Today is the perfect day to start.

Spiritual Capacity

Spiritual capacity is about who we are and what we want most in life. While the term *spiritual* is often put in a religious context, it means something different in the context of capacity building. Building spiritual capacity requires us to deeply evaluate what is most important to us, including defining our core values and delving into our purpose.

This is, of course, easier said than done. Growing this capacity requires dedicated reflection and deep self-awareness. Self-awareness is the foundation of personal and professional leadership. We cannot inspire, motivate, and guide others until we understand what is important to us and are consistent in our thoughts and actions.

On a deeper level, building spiritual capacity means truly getting to know ourselves and aligning our lives based on that knowledge. One of the scariest things about building spiritual capacity is it removes any excuses—once we know what we want most, it feels especially disappointing not to pursue it.

Though many of us are unaware of our core values and purpose, they are always with us. On a subconscious level, they drive the important decisions in our lives. When you make an important choice that aligns to your purpose and values, you feel confident and fulfilled. When you make a decision that goes against those same principles, it will feel unsatisfying or discomforting, even if you can't articulate why.

Capacity building starts with this area. If you don't know what you want most, you may waste a lot of time and energy running in the wrong direction. I didn't develop this capacity until I was well into my thirties, and it was then that I realized how many times I had burned myself out by being misaligned with my purpose and values.

The stories in these upcoming pages will help you reflect on the beliefs you hold that are nonnegotiable and guide you in clarifying your long-term vision.

There are a few questions to consider as you read these stories. When do you feel you are at your best? What type of environments and people make you feel energized? What causes are you willing to sacrifice for personally in order to help them advance?

As you read these stories, it may help to take notes on what stories resonate with you most and jot down your answers to the above questions. Discovering your core values is hard work, but doing this work will free you to spend more time doing things that fulfill you and empower you to move other things off your plate. You can use your core values as guideposts to make quicker, more confident decisions and understand which commitments and relationships in your life are most important.

It can be uncomfortable to peel back the layers of the onion and understand who we each really are at our core. But doing so will be the foundation of all lasting changes you can make in your life. Start today.

Raising Values

Recently, while reading Adam Grant's book *Originals*, I learned about a sociological study centered in one European town that compared two groups of neighbors: non-Jews who risked their lives to save Jews during the Holocaust (rescuers) and non-Jews who did nothing (non-rescuers).

The study revealed that what ultimately differentiated the rescuers from the non-rescuers was how their parents disciplined bad behavior and praised good behavior.

When the rescuers were asked to recall their childhoods and the discipline they received, researchers discovered that the word they most frequently used was "explained." Their parents focused on the *why* behind their disciplinary action and the moral lesson or value to be learned rather than on the discipline itself.

This practice conveyed the values their parents wanted to share while also encouraging critical thinking and reasoning. Grant notes that by explaining moral principles, the parents of those in the rescuer group had instilled in their children the importance of complying voluntarily with rules that aligned with important values and questioning rules that didn't.

The rescuers were almost three times more likely to reference moral values that applied to all people, emphasizing that their parents taught them to respect all human beings.

> "The moral values, ethical codes, and laws that guide our choices in normal times are, if anything, even more important to help us navigate the confusing and disorienting time of a disaster."
>
> **—SHERI FINK**

Another key to creating these high moral standards is praising behavior or character over the action itself. For example, in one study, children who were asked to be "helpers" instead of "to help" were more likely to clean up toys when asked. Similarly, adults who were told "Please don't be a cheater" cheated 50 percent less than those who were told "Please don't cheat."

It turns out that values are far more effective than rules at eliciting desired outcomes and behaviors. In either a family or an organization, it is virtually impossible to cover all possible rules or monitor the adherence to them. Doing so would create a lengthy process manual or a draconian set of guidelines.

I've observed that highly successful families, communities, and companies select and focus on a few values that are most important to them. These aren't token values that sit on the wall. They explain the why behind those values to their group and regularly reinforce them, both in terms of holding members to account for not meeting the standard as well as celebrating decisions made that support those values.

These values can cover hundreds, if not thousands, of situations, far more than any set of rules could. Most importantly, people are encouraged to openly question decisions or actions that are incongruous with the values. Enforcement is not top down; it's made by all the members of the group. The individuals who acted bravely to save would-be victims of the Holocaust were never explicitly told to do that. It was following the values that were instilled and strengthened throughout their lives that brought them to a logical, courageous decision.

Moment of Clarity

In 2018, I attended a conference session titled "Getting Clarity," led by world-renowned clarity coach Philip McKernan. Sitting in a circle, our group discussion began with a participant sharing that he'd been struggling with the decision about whether to sell his business. When McKernan asked him if he liked his business, his response was that he hadn't enjoyed coming to work for years. When asked what he would do next if he sold his business, he replied, "I don't know," to which McKernan responded, "But if you did know, what would that be?"

Right away, the seemingly indecisive business owner answered that he'd like to start a new career in a new industry. Minutes later, he'd committed to the entire group to start the process of selling his business and moving toward getting established in his desired career. The emotional relief on his face was visible.

Over the next few days, many similar conversations with McKernan took place, including my own. The reality for most of us is that while we know what we want, we are often afraid to even acknowledge it, much less pursue it.

Instead, we tell ourselves that we'll continue down our current path until we reach a specific financial milestone or some goal. Then, once that happens, we'll buckle down and

> "One of the scariest things in the world is to stand in front of the mirror and meet yourself."
>
> **—PHILIP MCKERNAN**

focus on what we really want to do. The problem with that line of thinking is that it's a slippery slope. We tend to keep moving the bar forward.

The sad truth is that although clarity lies within each of us, many of us don't actually want it. Gaining clarity might mean that we have to face a relationship that, in our gut, we know is doomed or move on from a career that isn't going anywhere or doesn't fulfill us.

McKernan's work inspired him to start an initiative called One Last Talk (OLT), a process in which regular people deliver a ten- to fifteen-minute talk as if it were the last talk they'd ever give before leaving this world. As you can imagine, these talks are intensely personal. It requires the person to both understand and be willing to share their truth. That truth is what drives a passion or purpose in life.

What McKernan has found with OLT is that people's first versions are typically about something universal or perfunctory, not about their story. Where it ends up after going

Listen to my interview with McKernan on *The Elevate Podcast*

9

through the OLT process is usually completely different and includes perspectives and stories that most have never shared publicly.

Just as McKernan requests of his OLT participants, my question to you is what story or stories are you holding on to that don't serve you? Are you ready to see the truth that lies beyond them?

Beautiful Day

A few years back, I noticed that my personal trainer, Mike Sirani, had a tattoo of the phrase "Beautiful Day" on the inside of his right bicep. Not figuring him for a U2 fan, I asked him about it. He explained that this phrase appeared often throughout the journals his grandfather kept for over twenty years. It was only after Mike's grandfather Paul Martino passed away that his family discovered the journals—mementos that have since become both a gift and treasure to them.

During his adult life, Mike's grandfather was in charge of all building and grounds maintenance at Sterling-Winthrop Research Institute in Rensselaer, NY. He was very proud of his job and was a good provider for his family. He also had great appreciation for the little things in life…trees, flowers, change in seasons, gardens.

At age fifty-nine, Paul was diagnosed with stage four non-Hodgkin's lymphoma. After chemo and a bone marrow transplant, he was cancer free for about one and a half years. Sadly, it returned, and at the young age of sixty-two, Paul passed away. During his chemo, it was discovered that other Sterling employees had succumbed to the same type of cancer, likely a result of their work environment, which involved both asbestos removal and exposure to radioactive rooms.

> "Carve your name on hearts, not tombstones. A legacy is etched into the minds of others and the stories they share about you."
>
> **— SHANNON L. ALDER**

"Beautiful Day" stood out to Mike in reading the journals because even when his grandfather wrote that he was "so tired," or that the temperature was below zero, or that it rained all day, or that he didn't feel well, he would often still write "Beautiful Day."

Paul's continued optimism in the face of adversity has left its mark on future generations of his family. It's affected how they've chosen to live their lives and approach situations, even adverse ones. Making this type of impact beyond our lifetime is something many never accomplish, despite having great means and opportunity.

What's important to remember is that it's never too early to begin thinking about your own legacy and how you will make an impact beyond your lifetime. For inspiration, read this incredibly eulogy on my website: fridayfwd.com/eulogy.

From personal experience, I and many others owe a debt of gratitude to Brian Brault, who served as global chair of Entrepreneur's Organization. Brian has cemented his own legacy by helping inspire a future generation of entrepreneurs to contemplate and create theirs. At a recent entrepreneurial leadership class, Brian started off his session with the question, "How do you want to be remembered in one hundred years?"

Answering such a question can be a very difficult exercise. It forces you to honestly examine your life, how you want to be remembered, and the values that you want to see carried on in future generations. In this process, many people realize that they are not living in a way that reflects the legacy they want to leave and that they need to make major changes.

So what do you want people to say about you in one hundred years?

Wishing Happiness

"I just want my ____ (child, spouse, employee, etc.) to be happy" is something we often hear but don't often see demonstrated with equal conviction. In reality, these words tend to default to our own judgment and definitions of what happiness is and means. If we truly and authentically wanted the people we cared about to be happy, we would support them more, judge them less, and accept them for who they are. In the words of a survivor of US Airways 1549, which after takeoff lost power in both engines and landed safely on the Hudson River in NYC, "We also might choose 'happiness' over being 'right.'"

The inspiration for this message comes from an incredibly moving piece written by Amy Krouse Rosenthal. It is titled "You May Want to Marry My Husband." In September 2015, Amy was diagnosed with terminal ovarian cancer. In her beautiful article, she managed to write a tribute to her husband that was also an open advertisement for someone to make him as happy after she was gone as he had made her.

Sadly, Amy passed away in 2017, but her story taught me an invaluable lesson about what it really means to wish happiness for others who we care about—selfless happiness, without strings attached and without making it about ourselves. Her story is also a powerful reminder that life is short. Choosing to

> "All the happiness there is in this world comes from thinking about others, and all the suffering comes from preoccupation with yourself."
>
> **— SHANTIDEVA**

live via a "deferred life plan"—putting off embracing opportunities and happiness until a later point—might not work out as planned.

Whether or not it was a coincidence, shortly after reading Amy's article, my family and I made some decisions about how to go about tackling some items on our bucket list this year and these became some of our best memories together.

So the next time you say "I just want _____ to be happy," think about Amy and her story and truly ask yourself if your actions match your words.

Myth of Work-Life Balance

People often talk about wanting work-life balance, but I don't believe it is what they are really seeking—the concept itself is fundamentally unachievable. Many people's concept of what a perfectly balanced professional and personal life looks like often leads to subpar outcomes, disappointment, and frustrations because it's based on time allocation and trying to do too many things at once. In trying too hard to "balance" their schedule, they are checking off the boxes but not getting the best outcomes due to an approach that is quantitative versus qualitative.

Rather than balance, what I believe we really want is the ability to be truly present in our work and in our lives outside work. We are seeking meaningful, uninterrupted, "all in" experiences at each end of the work/life spectrum, which will naturally cycle at different times. There often won't be balance within a week or a day, and hours aren't the determinant of quality.

In the end, the goal is not balance in the traditional sense; it's a life that lets you integrate those pieces. Work-life integration is more akin to a puzzle where all the different pieces fit together in aggregate. It's an understanding that each day or week might bring a different combination of things to attend to at work or in your personal life, but they total a portfolio of

> "There is no such thing as work-life balance. Everything worth fighting for unbalances your life."

—ALAIN DE BOTTON

quality experiences. It's not about the time itself; it's about being fully present and engaged in each of the pieces.

For the next week, try and measure your success at home and at work by the amount of quality, uninterrupted experiences you are able to have rather than trying to find an unachievable balance. I believe you will feel more satisfied and accomplished all around.

Freedom to Fail

We all need room to make mistakes. The goal should be to learn from them and move forward without repeating them. An example of restricting that freedom is Volkswagen's diesel engine debacle, which was uncovered in 2015. According to many company executives, former CEO Martin Winterkorn was demanding and authoritarian, and he abhorred failure; he also fostered a climate of fear.

A key part of Volkswagen's aggressive growth strategy was a new diesel engine that would deliver low emissions and high efficiency, the automotive Holy Grail, if you will. The problem was that as the engine came into production, it didn't meet the goals Winterkorn had publicly stated it would. Too afraid to bring this failure to their boss, the engineers used their collective ingenuity to cover up the problem, leading to billions of dollars in losses and damage to the brand.

A great example of a leader embracing failure can be found in Ray Dalio's bestselling book, *Principles*. In it, Ray speaks about an expensive oversight that an employee made at his hedge fund and his decision not to fire the person. Ray believed that firing the employee would encourage others to conceal their mistakes out of fear.

Instead, Ray used the experience to create a "mistake log"

> "The greatest successes come from having the freedom to fail."

—MARK ZUCKERBERG

where all mistakes were reported and logged company-wide so others could learn from them. Now, making mistakes is not a fireable offense. However, failing to report a mistake is.

The concept of failure is a nuanced one with many cultural implications. But ask any successful person and they'll tell you how failure and learning from it contributed to or was the cause of their success. Sadly, so many parents today are robbing their children of this valuable experience.

Sure, these helicopter parents may be well-intentioned, but they are grossly overreaching. Because they can't handle seeing their kids truly be challenged, uncomfortable, or, god forbid, failures at something, they interfere in every area of their lives.

I strongly believe that this explicit and implicit discouragement of failure poses a serious and growing threat for the development of an entire generation, an opinion shared by many others.

Man with a Plan

One of my favorite writing themes is to debunk the myth of the overnight success. Ed Sheeran fits this mold to a T.

At fourteen years old, Sheeran began performing in London and convinced his parents to let him move there at just seventeen to continue writing and singing. He apparently played in three hundred live shows over four years and sold self-published CDs from a rucksack without any real success. Along the way, he lost his apartment and resorted to couch surfing at friends' homes and even sleeping in public transport and near a heating duct outside Buckingham Palace. He reflected on those times in a recent interview, saying:

"There were moments I wanted to give up. The nights that you don't have a couch to sleep on or you don't have money in your pocket, or food in your stomach, or a charged phone, those become the nights where you reassess your situation."

But he didn't give up. In fact, he forged ahead. In April 2010, he bought a one-way ticket to Los Angeles with one contact and no money, just the hope and will that he'd get discovered. He continued his couch surfing and played open mic nights all over the city. But eventually, he got his big break.

From there, his career started to take off. His first album, +, was followed by his second album, ×, and his third album, ÷.

|| "Success is the best revenge for anything."

—ED SHEERAN

Sheeran disclosed that this was the naming plan for his albums all along, leaving little doubt for me that his next album will be called "–," continuing his mathematical album naming sequence and his commitment to live out the plan he envisioned for himself.

There is no doubt Ed Sheeran has tremendous talent, but so do many other artists—all of whom have similar aspirations to make it big. So in addition to his talent, what's led to his stratospheric success? Some familiar themes emerge. He had a clear vision and a plan; he had an incredible work ethic; he had dogged determination and persistence to see his dream through, despite failures, fatigue, disappointments, and setbacks. He was willing to take risks and bet on himself, and he's remained humble throughout it all.

Last but not least, Sheeran did not give himself a safety net to fall back on. Plan A (success as a musician) was his only option. Maybe he was just following the advice of his father, who once told him, "If you really want to do it, don't have a fallback plan. Because you eventually will do it if there's no other option."

Either way, the man had a plan.

Having Potential

Much of our motivation in life is driven by two feelings that are often at different ends of the emotional spectrum: inspiration and discomfort.

This week, the focus is on discomfort.

Recently, a friend of mine, Conor Neill, spoke to a group and imparted some harsh but salient wisdom that stuck with me. He said, "When you are ten, potential is cute. When you are twenty, it's nice. But by the time you get to forty, it starts to become an insult."

While this can be painful for some to hear, there's a lot of truth in his words. As time goes on, using that same phrase moves from something inspiring to something that becomes a crutch to, eventually, an insult.

Don't believe me? Tell a mom or dad of a fifteen-year-old that they have the potential to be a great parent and see how they react.

It's not that a person who has been dabbling in something for ten to twenty years without success doesn't have potential. What's more likely is that they lack the talent or the conviction to convert that potential into something meaningful.

Realistically, potential has an expiration date.

|| "There is no heavier burden than a great potential."

—CHARLES SCHULZ

Ultimately, we need to decide where we want to convert our potential into achievement. These will likely be areas in your life that are most important to you, not what others decide are most important or valuable.

The question to think about in your own life or organization is where in the future would it be an insult to look back and hear that you had had potential?

I have asked myself this very question. At no point in my life do I want to look back and feel that I had the potential to be or do better—as a father, a husband, or a leader in my business—and not lived up to it.

With that in mind, pretend it's five years from now and ask yourself the following:

- Where would I not want to be told I had potential in my business (either overall or for a product)?
- Where would I not want to be told I had potential in my family and personal life?
- Where would I be really upset to hear that I had the potential to be an X?

If you're not on track to live up to your potential in any of these areas, then go do something about it.

Don't be someone who had potential. Be someone who acted on their potential.

A Dad's Influence

Years ago, Natan Parsons, a mentor and colleague, told me that he knew his kids would do stupid things and make bad decisions, but that was all part of life. Ultimately, he only cared if they were "good people" who contributed positively to society in some way. For him, it was about core values, first and foremost, and this is where he chose to fight his battles, especially in the context of his own hard-fought battle with cancer, which he eventually lost.

I am often reminded of this lesson, such as last week when I argued with my teenage daughter about her Instagram use and messy room, only to then have her ask me to donate half the money she made selling T-shirts to benefit the victims of the Manchester, UK, bombing. Sometimes we overlook the forest for the trees.

I have found one of the most powerful aspects of being a father is seeing the world through the eyes of my children. That lens has become a critical filter for decision-making and thinking about the examples I want to set. It also serves to remind us that the "do as I say, not as I do" method of parenting or leadership will eventually hit a wall. My kids have become quite good at pointing out my own hypocrisies (i.e., "Dad, put your phone down!").

One of the most popular topics I've discussed is the false premise of work-life balance, the notion that we should be able to

> "A hundred years from now it will not matter what my bank account was, the sort of house I lived in, or the kind of car I drove. But the world may be different because I was important in the life of a child."
>
> **—FOREST E. WITCRAFT**

perfectly balance our personal and professional responsibilities. Rather than balance, I believe what we really want is the ability to be truly present in our work and in our lives outside work—especially with our families. This includes having meaningful, uninterrupted, "all in" experiences.

Scott Weiss, founder of IronPort Systems, wrote a great article related to this titled "My Success at Work Made Me a Failure at Home." In it, he shares some practical advice from his own experience trying to "do it all," which included four principles for better engaging with his family.

1. Disconnect to connect
2. Planning and priorities
3. Communication
4. Participation

For many of us, being a parent will be the most important and impactful job that we ever have.

Moon Shot

From a historical perspective, one of the greatest examples of overcoming impossible goals is President John F. Kennedy's declaration in 1962 that the United States would put a man on the surface of the moon before the end of the decade. At the time, this goal seemed unfathomable to most.

In his acclaimed book *Built to Last: Successful Habits of Visionary Companies*, Jim Collins coined the term BHAG, which stands for Big Hairy Audacious Goal.

Collins wrote: "A BHAG engages people—it reaches out and grabs them in the gut. It is tangible, energizing, highly focused. People 'get it' right away; it takes little or no explanation."

From a historical perspective, one of the greatest examples of a BHAG is President John F. Kennedy's declaration in 1962 that the United States would put a man on the surface of the moon before the end of the decade. At the time, this goal seemed unfathomable to most.

2020 marked the fiftieth anniversary of that goal coming to fruition: the spaceflight Apollo 11 landing humans on the moon on July 20, 1969, and allowing Neil Armstrong and Buzz Aldrin to be the first humans to step foot on another planetary body. The third astronaut, Michael Collins, remained in the command module to ensure their safety.

> "We choose to go to the moon in this decade and do the other things, not because they are easy, but because they are hard, because that goal will serve to organize and measure the best of our energies and skills."
>
> **—PRESIDENT JOHN F. KENNEDY**

The media coverage commemorating this incredible event has provided insight into the extensive planning, financial commitment, vision, and teamwork that was required to make this extraordinary achievement possible. It's also shed light on three important takeaways that any organization can learn from.

Where There Is a Will, There Is a Way

One fact that I'm personally astounded by is that an iPhone has one hundred thousand times more processing power than the Apollo 11's onboard computer. To put this in context, this means that an iPhone today could handle 120 million moon missions at once. So clearly, it's not always about having the best technology, the right tools, or the smartest people; it's about having the individual and collective will.

Specific and Measurable Goals

Had Kennedy said that the United States should "enhance its space capabilities" by the end of the decade, it is very unlikely that humans would have landed on the moon. The more inspiring, specific, and time-sensitive something is, the more likely others will rally together toward achieving it.

Dream Team

To achieve those first lunar footsteps, everyone needed to understand that they were part of one team with one goal, regardless of their expertise or success in the marketplace.

For example, the hundreds of private vendors who were awarded the contracts to handle key elements of the Apollo 11 technology were competitors outside the program. However, inside the program, they were part of one team. This was a remarkable example of industry competitors coming together to create an all-star team for a bigger purpose.

What was also apparent from the Apollo 11 anniversary media coverage is that experts from all over the world—mathematicians, engineers, scientists, mechanics, technicians, pilots, and thousands of others who worked tirelessly behind the scenes—all set aside their egos in pursuit of that common goal. The Apollo 11 program proves that, when we don't allow ourselves or our teams to put personal or team-centered needs above the needs of the organization as a whole, we can accomplish amazing feats.

Breaking Bad

To be great, organizations and individuals alike need to embrace their bad side. I don't mean bad in the behavioral sense. I mean being clear about what you're not going to be good at.

This was a key message Frances (Fran) Frei gave in her presentation to an audience of business leaders that I attended. Fran, a bestselling author and speaker on leadership and customer service, shared a few examples, such as IKEA. When establishing themselves, IKEA created a new market for furniture by deciding to be bad at assembly, quality, and convenience of store locations. Instead, they focused on being great on price, systems, and stylish furniture created for small spaces. By targeting buyers who wanted the latter and cared less about the former, they've built revenues that exceeded $40 billion in 2019.

We each face similar decisions in our personal and professional lives. More often than not, we try to do many things well rather than figuring out the handful of things we're good at that are most important. Once we've figured out what those select things are, we should be unapologetic about being bad at things that fall outside that.

Trying to be good at everything just doesn't work.

In her talk, Fran shared another example of working parents she had studied and the differences in their happiness levels. The

> "Choosing bad is your only shot at achieving greatness.
> And resisting it is a recipe for mediocrity."
>
> **—FRANCES FREI**

ones who were unhappy and stressed were trying to be good at everything in their lives simultaneously. The ones who were happier were clearer about the things they had the bandwidth to be good at (e.g., their jobs, their family relationships, etc.). They were also more willing to let other things fall by the wayside, either permanently or temporarily. In other words, they had unapologetically embraced being bad at them.

One of the first steps on this path is giving up the guilt about what you are bad at. Even though I have written a lot about the important of excellence, breaking the habit of feeling guilt about things I'm bad at is something I've been working on improving. By playing to my strengths, I've been able to have a bigger impact on my employees, my friends, and my family.

It never feels natural to be bad. What's important to remember is that it's in the service of being great at things that matter more. Remember, if you try to be everything to everyone, you will just end up being nothing to no one.

Purpose and Pain

I once attended a Mastermind Dinner in NYC on the topic of work-life integration. The host had hired a sketch artist to create a visual representation of our discussion so that each attendee could have a unique and interesting reminder of the discussion to take with them.

Intrigued by her skill, I asked the artist how she'd gotten into this line of work, to which she replied, "My purpose is to allow people to be fully seen and heard."

Struck by the clarity of her answer, I asked her if that purpose came from a personal place or from her childhood (prefaced by saying that it was fine not to answer if she felt my question was too personal). Without hesitating, she replied that she'd had a severe stutter as a child and struggled to communicate.

While inspired, I was not surprised by her answer. In hearing many high achievers talk about why they do what they do, the consistent pattern I've detected is that one's purpose often stems from a formative life experience, commonly a painful one.

For example, someone who had a difficult time learning to read as a child might be driven to become a champion of literacy. Or someone whose family suffered a major injustice is more likely to become an advocate of the law or human rights.

Many of us are held back because we don't fully recognize or

> "I do believe to my core...that our greatest gifts lie right next to our deepest wounds."

—PHILIP MCKERNAN

lean into the pain that transformed itself into our core purpose or passion. Instead, we avoid or deny a reality because we don't want to place blame on others or be seen as a victim.

For example, consider someone who creates an award-winning afterschool program because they'd had a single parent who worked two jobs and wasn't around much. That person's ability to appreciate that their parent did the best they could to provide for them is mutually exclusive from honoring how being alone so often made them feel.

The relationship between purpose and pain also implies that pain is an important ingredient in our personal and professional development. Today's leaders often struggle to let their employees make mistakes and experience discomfort. For example, I know many new managers who got far more serious about refining their interviewing process after making a bad hiring decision. It was a necessary part of their development and a lesson they will likely carry with them throughout their career due to the negative impact it had on their teams.

The tragedy of this avoidance of discomfort and pain is that it's ultimately robbing the person of experiences that could lead to their greatest transformation and discovery of their core purpose.

This week, reflect back on your childhood or career. Is there an experience(s) that has been driving you consciously or unconsciously for years? Are you missing the obvious connection?

Maybe it's time to use that to your advantage.

Carpe Diem

Carpe diem is Latin for "seize the day." It means to make the most of the present time and give little thought to the future.

When I was given the opportunity to attend the Super Bowl for the first time, my instinct was to stay at home and avoid the chaos, but the historical implications of the game got the better of me. My oldest son, whose bedroom is a shrine to Tom Brady, also gave me a lot of "subtle" hints about how much he wanted to go with me. He had actually prominently featured a picture of Tom Brady holding the championship trophy on his vision board, which each family member created for themselves New Year's Day.

In the weeks leading up to the game, he had numerous dreams about the Super Bowl. He'd share them with me in the morning and most of them included him being at the game. Something in the back of my mind told me that this was an experience we should have together, so I started looking around for a ticket for him.

No luck. Then, a few days before the game, a ticket became available. However, when I went to check for flights, they were all sold out.

As I said my goodbye to him on my way to the airport, I gave him a hug and told him that I was sorry it didn't work out and

|| "I have no regrets. I don't think you can afford to."

—ALUN WYN JONES

that perhaps it just wasn't meant to be (something an eleven-year-old really doesn't want to hear).

As I sat in the airport waiting for my flight, something prompted me to check the Delta app one last time. Suddenly, a low-level award ticket was available—the last seat on the plane. I bought it immediately as I had twenty-four hours to cancel.

On my flight to Houston, I contacted everyone I knew in my network and, to my surprise, I secured him a very reasonable ticket to the game. Everything was falling into place. However, as I sat in the Houston airport ready to make the final call to purchase his game ticket, I thought to myself, "This is nuts. I am forty-one and this is my first Super Bowl. At eleven, he'd have to fly alone to meet me. He may be too young for this experience. We should wait. There will be other opportunities." Honestly, I was seconds away from calling the whole thing off.

Suddenly, I thought back to a quote I had used just a few weeks earlier: "We only regret the chances we didn't take." As a person who always emphasizes the importance of living without regrets, I knew if threw in the towel, I'd be a hypocrite. So I called my wife and said, "I am sorry for the work this puts on you, but let's do it. I just have a feeling about this." My son decided it was as good of a time as any to take his first flight alone.

My son and I, along with his grandfather, got to witness the greatest Super Bowl game and comeback in history. One day, I hope to tell my grandkids about being at the game with their dad where we saw the Edelman "ankle catch" and where Tom Brady and Bill Belichick broke the NFL records.

I can tell you with absolute certainty that, had the Patriots lost the game, I would have had no regrets. It would have stung, but the experience itself would have been worth the trip. We actually talked about that as the game headed into the fourth quarter. But had I known I had the opportunity and decided to pass on it, that certainly would have haunted me for years. Regret, really, is rarely about what we do. It's about what we don't, should have, or didn't do.

In my eyes, the real hero in this story is a very determined eleven-year-old who had a vision and was committed to seeing it through. Then, when presented with the opportunity of a lifetime, he got over any fears he must have had, got on that plane, and seized the day. That's a valuable lesson for all of us.

Intellectual Capacity

If spiritual capacity dictates the big-picture characteristics that guide your life decisions, intellectual capacity establishes the day-to-day actions that advance you toward your purpose. Intellectual capacity relates to how you think, learn, plan, and execute with discipline.

Intellectual capacity ultimately boils down to your mindset, planning, and daily actions. It sounds simple, but the first step of building intellectual capacity is believing you can. A consistent quality of most high performers is intellectual curiosity—they've expanded their capabilities by always wanting to learn more and seeking out new information.

If you think of your intellectual capacity as fixed, you won't be able to get better. Adopting a growth mindset and proactively seeking opportunities to learn is crucial to building intellectual capacity. This also means soliciting direct feedback and hearing honest input about where you need to improve and your blind spots.

Intellectual capacity is also built around setting clear goals and establishing the disciplined habits needed to reach them. Goal setting is only effective when we set long-term goals and design our short-term goals to build toward them. Otherwise, we will just be checking boxes on a to-do list without leading toward anything meaningful. We often fall into a routine of prioritizing urgent things over important ones.

The last facet of intellectual capacity is perhaps the most difficult to build—instilling consistent, proactive actions into our day-to-day lives. For me, this meant dedicating myself to the morning routine that led to the creation of Friday Forward. It also meant allocating time to learn about the areas I needed to improve most to reach my goals. I spent time reading, listening to podcasts from experts, and participating in peer organizations where I could consistently learn from others.

In today's fast-paced world, it can be tempting to dismiss your efforts if you don't dramatically improve in a short amount of time. Intellectual capacity is about getting just a little better each day—small gains that compound over time.

The stories in this section reinforce this idea and provide inspiration to build these steady improvements into your life. You'll learn why the idea of "overnight success" is very misleading. You'll understand how to differentiate between tasks that are important in the long term and urgent in the short term. You'll be inspired by people who commit to excellence in everything they do and go the extra mile for others. You will walk away with many ideas about how to make proactive changes starting today.

As you read, it's helpful to consider these questions: What goals have you set, and why are they important? Who are the people in your life who can give you honest feedback and hold you accountable? What are new things you want to learn but haven't set aside time to study? What are good habits you want to start or bad habits you want to kick?

There isn't a shortcut to building intellectual capacity—it takes time and commitment. But the examples shared in the following pages will demonstrate why doing this will help you excel professionally and personally. If it feels like you never have enough time, you will certainly see the value in getting more of the right things done in that same twenty-four-hour day we are all given.

Myth of the Overnight Success

Years ago, I had the pleasure of hearing Uri Levine, cofounder of Waze, speak to a small group. The popular social navigation app had just been sold to Google for $1.15 billion. At the time, the rumor on the street was that Google had bought Waze a year into their existence. I'll admit that when I first heard that rumor, my initial thought was, what a lucky ba**ard. But I should have known better.

From Uri's story, it became evident that Waze was not an overnight success. In fact, it was more of a decade-long struggle with several near-death experiences that left the management team with very little equity. Fortunately, the company was driven by a founder (Uri) who has an incredible passion for solving logistical issues—so much so that he usually wears a T-shirt that says, "Fall in love with the problem, not the solution."

Since hearing Uri speak, I've read several similar stories that continue to debunk the myth of the overnight success, including that of Ben Silbermann. Ben stuck with his pet project after a year of failures, declining traffic, and a lack of understanding about his product from friends and family. What kept him going was a genuine passion for his idea combined with a fear of failure and embarrassment. His grit paid off, and now most of us are familiar with or use what became of his pet project: Pinterest.

|| "Intelligence without ambition is a bird without wings."

—ANONYMOUS

So why does the myth of the overnight success seem to perpetuate? Perhaps because it's often easier for us to ascribe success to luck or timing as opposed to passion, dogged determination, or thousands of hours of hard work and grit. It's similar to when someone tries to excuse laziness or underachievement by remarking in their defense that the person is "smart," as if that entitles them to success. It's far better to recognize someone's work ethic rather than their intelligence. The truth is nothing worth doing is easy.

We should stop permitting excuses and stories that mask what it really takes to achieve success, simply because we may be too afraid to make that investment ourselves. The next time you hear about an overnight success story, dig a little deeper. Most are decades in the making.

Sharing Belief

Having people in our lives who share their belief in us is incredibly important; it's the underpinning of great leadership, good parenting, and many religious foundations.

That said, belief must also be coupled with reality; reality of what it will take to achieve the desired outcome. One without the other will likely lead to failure, disappointment, and even unreached potential.

For example, I can tell my daughter that I believe she can get into Harvard or become an Olympian, but that should be accompanied by an explanation of what that will require in terms of passion, skills, effort, commitment, and time. She must know that if she really wants something, no one else can or should do the work for her.

This dynamic is behind my own parenting philosophy, which is "you can have anything you desire if you are willing to do what's required."

Belief grounded in reality is critical. It's also something I think many micromanagers and helicopter parents get very wrong. Telling someone that you believe in them and then doing the work for them at the first sign of struggle doesn't allow them to gain the experience of learning from their own mistakes, which is an essential element of success.

> "Sometimes you have to believe in the belief others have in you until your belief kicks in."
>
> **—JOHN DIJULIUS**

Let's all remember the power of inspiring others to build their capacity without actually doing the work for them. Be there to root them on and then stay out of their way as they learn to believe in themselves.

Urgent vs. Important

A powerful priority-setting tool made famous by author Steven Covey is called Eisenhower's urgent-important principle. As its name suggests, this is a tool used by President Dwight Eisenhower to identify tasks and activities that demanded his attention and those that he should either ignore or designate as lower priority.

According to this principle, our tasks will typically fall into one of four quadrants. We also tend to complete them in this order:

1. Urgent and important
2. Urgent and not important
3. Important and not urgent
4. Not urgent and not important

A common productivity mistake is not focusing energy on important and not urgent before urgent and not important. The problem with this approach is that if you keep ignoring the important things you want to accomplish long term, you set yourself up to be reactive when those things eventually become both urgent and important; this is firefighting mode.

Prioritizing things that are urgent and not important also

> "What is important is seldom urgent and what is urgent is seldom important."
>
> **—UNKNOWN, AS QUOTED BY PRESIDENT DWIGHT EISENHOWER**

distracts you from taking action toward what is most important. In essence, the squeaky wheel gets the grease. While it can feel good to cross seemingly urgent items off your list, they don't really move the needle in your personal or professional life.

A year ago, I began organizing my to-do list into the following buckets and recommended order:

1. **Important and urgent:** Firefighting and necessity.
2. **Important, not urgent:** Opportunity, strategy, and values-oriented projects.
3. **Urgent, not important:** Avoid interruptions and busy work, and limit investment or delegate where possible.
4. **Not important or urgent:** Eliminate and ignore the trivial and wasteful.

I have also talked to many others who have done the same and have experienced great results. When I follow this to-do list process, I find that I am able to meet my goals with fewer things sneaking up on me.

The notion I want to leave you with is if we live our lives in a reactionary way, we will never accomplish the bigger goals we set for ourselves. Whether you choose to use Eisenhower's urgent/important principle or some other productivity tool, the key is to avoid the urgent distractions and stay focused on what you want to achieve in the long term. If you do, you'll find yourself accomplishing so much more than you thought possible.

Early Riser

When the global financial crisis hit in 2008, Hal Elrod experienced a professional near-death experience. His speaking engagements and coaching clients canceled their contracts. He had just bought a house and gotten engaged, and without that income, he quickly racked up $425,000 in debt. He was on a downhill spiral and openly contemplated suicide.

Needing some motivation and inspiration, he began studying some of the world's highest achievers (artists, athletes, business leaders, etc.). What he noticed was that almost all of them had a morning routine that shared a few similar elements.

Not sure which ones to focus on, Elrod decided to develop his own personal morning routine that incorporated all the elements and, with the help of his wife, coined his new sunup ritual "The Miracle Morning." Eventually, he wrote about his morning routine and how it turned his life around. A short time later, his book, *The Miracle Morning,* became a bestseller and garnered a loyal online and offline community of productive early risers.

I started incorporating the Miracle Morning habits into my life a few years ago and have not looked back.

Here are the six key elements of a meaningful morning routine, which Hal coined his Life SAVERS:

> "If you take care of your mornings, the rest of your life takes care of itself."
>
> **—HAL ELROD**

1. **Silence.** This can be meditation, prayer, reflection, deep breathing, or expressions of gratitude done individually or in combination with other steps.

2. **Affirmation:** Repeating positive statements about oneself in order to create a positive, self-confident attitude.

3. **Visualization:** Using your imagination to create mental pictures of specific outcomes and behaviors that you are hoping to achieve.

4. **Exercise.** Even just a few minutes to get your blood pumping and heart rate elevated. It has so many positive benefits related to stress, focus, and more.

5. **Reading.** At least ten pages a day on a topic focused on personal development or inspiration. You can even use this book.

6. **Scribing.** Writing each day, whether in a journal, pages for a book, or just stream of consciousness. Hal actually wrote *The Miracle Morning* during his morning routine, and it's how I've done most of my writing for articles and books.

In 2016, Hal was diagnosed with an aggressive form of cancer that had only a 30 percent survival rate. He beat that too and now speaks about the critical role that his established Miracle Morning routine played in his cancer battle and remission.

If you do the same research that Hal did, you will find that almost anyone with sustained achievement at a high level—and who is not a night owl—has a morning routine. They get up early and play offense rather than react defensively to the world around them. They start each day with intention and focus on what's most important to them, not to everyone else. They run their days rather than having their days run them.

Most people insist that they just can't get up any earlier. I would argue, from my own experience, that you can't afford not to.

Being Lucky

Once in an interview, I was asked how much I believed that luck played into the success of our business over the years. It was a fair question. Sure, a lot of things have gone our way over the years, even when we didn't think they would, and we have also had some bad breaks. However, that only tells part of the story. Timing and preparedness played a key role in both.

My preferred definition of luck comes from this old adage: "Luck is what happens when preparation meets opportunity."

We all know people who seem to be habitually lucky, or unlucky, for that matter. How much of that is really in their control?

For instance, when the subprime mortgage crisis hit in 2008, some people owned multiple houses with interest-only mortgages—mortgages they really could not afford. They borrowed recklessly. Yet others saved during that time and waited patiently on the sidelines. They made the decision to not chase what became known as "irrational exuberance."

When the housing market crashed seemingly overnight and home prices fell 20 to 30 percent, people who borrowed recklessly would probably chalk up their losses to being "unlucky" or having "bad timing." Conversely, people in the second group, those who saved and waited during the subprime frenzy, were

> "Shallow men believe in luck... Strong men believe in cause and effect."
>
> **—RALPH WALDO EMERSON**

well positioned and probably felt that they were "lucky" or had "great timing." The same circumstance played out two different ways based on what preceded the event.

Looking at this notion through the lens of preparedness meeting opportunity better explains how a situation could be regarded as unlucky or lucky; it's often based on the prevailing circumstances.

There are certainly times when we just have "good" or "bad" luck—such as finding a $100 bill on the ground or being in the way of a bird that has great aim. But if we just credit every situation as either "good luck" or "bad luck" without considering our own choices and behavior, we do ourselves a disservice. What's more is that we may not learn from our mistakes or recognize how we created an opportunity for success.

So thinking back to the question I was asked, we've absolutely been lucky in many different situations. We've also made some good strategic decisions to position ourselves for success when the opportunity presented itself.

I'd like to think we can all create more of our own luck.

World Class

Ann Miura-Ko grew up as a first-generation American. Like millions before them, her parents immigrated to the United States in search of a better life and more opportunity. Miura-Ko's parents also had high expectations for their children. Her father, a rocket scientist at NASA, was passionate about the concept of excellence.

One of the principles Miura-Ko's father regularly repeated and instilled in her was the importance of giving a world-class effort in everything she did, no matter how trivial. From a very young age, he would always ask if her effort in virtually anything was "the best she could do."

After struggling with extreme shyness, the introverted Miura-Ko eventually developed into an elite high school debater. She went on to attend college at Yale and, while there, as part of her financial aid, secured a job as an administrative assistant in the office of the dean of engineering.

On the first day of work, she happened to call her parents to say hello, and her father reminded her to think about how she could be world-class in her new job. She explained to him that she would just be making copies and filing, but he responded with, "I think you should think about it."

Respecting his advice, she decided to rethink how she

|| "Whatever you are, be a good one."

—WILLIAM MAKEPEACE THACKERAY

approached her tasks. She focused on crisp copies that people could not discern from the original; she chose to use a label maker for filing, rather than hand write them; she even made sure to pick the freshest donuts when she was asked to bring them into the office.

Her stated goal was to make everything a "delight moment" for the people she worked with.

One day, a few years into Miura-Ko's job, the dean popped his head out of the office and told her that he needed someone to tour his friend Lewis around the engineering school.

Miura-Ko gave a great tour and developed a good rapport with the gentleman but had no idea who he was. At the end of the tour, he asked if she would like to come to California for a tour of her own during spring break, shadowing him at his company. It was then that she learned that "Lewis" was Lewis "Lew" Platt, CEO of Hewlett Packard.

Miura-Ko jumped at the opportunity and had a great experience. When she returned to campus, Lew sent her two pictures. The first one was of herself sitting next to Lew, talking to him. The second picture was of Bill Gates, who had also recently visited. He was sitting exactly where she had sat. This image left a lasting impression on her, and Platt became a key figure in her professional development.

Ann Miura-Ko has gone on to become one of the most respected venture capitalists in the country, playing a significant role in helping to shatter the glass ceiling for women in her industry. She's been referred to by *Forbes* as "the most powerful woman in startups."

While often incredibly challenging to execute, the wisdom imparted over and over by Miura-Ko's father was astute. When we commit to being excellent or world-class in all that we do, we are choosing to own our circumstances, no matter how insignificant they might seem at the time.

Is there sometimes just plain ol' luck involved? Sure. But if one of the top investors in the world got her break making copies, labeling, selecting fresh donuts, and demonstrating accountability, where in your daily routine might you be able to do better?

Stop-Doing List

For many of us, the first few weeks of the year are focused on goal creation and to-do lists for the developing year. While those are certainly important, I'd encourage you to add one more thing to your agenda that will likely contribute the most to your success this year: a stop-doing list.

The most successful people and businesses know how to focus on what needs to get done and what they need to stop doing in order to make that happen.

If you want to make room for new initiatives this year, then some old things need to go, including using "being busy" as an excuse for not getting the right things done.

Here are three areas that companies and individuals should consider when determining what to stop doing this year.

Tasks and Time Wasters

Take a hard look at specific tasks and activities you regularly engage in. The ones that exhaust you or feel like a chore should go. This may mean finding a grocery delivery service, removing Facebook from your phone or, in my case, finding a service that can take over paying 90 percent of my bills. You need to be honest with yourself about where your time is going and how it could be better spent so you can use your

> "If you want something new, you have to stop doing something old."
>
> **—PETER F. DRUCKER**

time and energy in ways that have more value and support your higher goals.

Commitments

Commitments are a level above tasks. They are the recurring investments of your time. They might include a committee you volunteer on, a class, or a regular get-together. Whatever they are, some may have run their course. Moving on from them can refocus and reenergize you, which allows you to allocate time, energy, and resources toward something new. For example, once I realized how valuable my morning routine is to my day and life, I stopped doing breakfast meetings altogether.

People

To quote Jim Rohn, "You are the average of the five people you spend the most time with." I can't think of a more powerful statement. One of the most important things you can do in this life is move away from relationships and people who no longer align with your values and direction. If you feel worse after spending time with someone, chances are they're an energy vampire (see page 115). Albeit difficult, it's likely time to pull away from them, even if they are family. This doesn't mean burning bridges; it just means that you stop engaging, making plans, or giving that relationship as much of your precious time and energy.

This week, as you add to your goals and to-do lists, take time to think about what you or your business needs to stop doing this year to be successful.

Power of Keystone Habits

I get a lot of great feedback and ideas about my weekly writing, but the most common question I receive is, "How do you keep it up each week?"

The answer to this question really has two parts. The first is that it's something I enjoy doing and that aligns with my core purpose (sharing ideas that help people and businesses grow). The second is that it has become a habit.

One of the more influential books I've read is Charles Duhigg's *The Power of Habit.* His book offers an amazing window into how to change behavior and habits in a lasting way. For example, did you know that it takes approximately twenty-one days of repetition to form a new habit?

One of Duhigg's most important principles is that there are keystone habits in our lives that, if changed, will lead to positive change in many other areas of our lives.

For example, people who commit to consistent exercise suddenly find themselves doing better in their other commitments. Likewise, people who were asked to keep a food journal for a study on different diets lost far more weight than those who didn't keep a food journal. The act of journaling turned out to have a significant influence on more than just diet itself.

Paul O'Neil, the legendary CEO of Alcoa, is best known for

> "If you believe you can change—if you make it a habit—the change becomes real."
>
> **—CHARLES DUHIGG**

turning around the company by getting everyone focused on safety. When employees saw the commitment and results from that consistent effort, everything else in the company started to improve.

The takeaway is that if you really want to hit your goals, find your keystone habit and build from there, and momentum will follow.

Life Hack

These days, everyone seems to be looking for a shortcut or a hack. Apparently, things like "growth hacking," "social media hacking," "biohacking" and so on are all the rage. It appears everyone wants to find that magical shortcut that will lead them to getting more output with less effort.

Recently, I came across a great post about useful hacks by Morgan Housel, a partner at Collaborative Fund. He wrote about attending a three-hour session with a social media consultant who walked attendees through a slew of social media–related hacks. However, although she talked about things like when to post and why to create hashtags, Housel notes that the trainer never actually talked about the most important component: creating good content to post.

I understand exactly where he's coming from. Good writing takes time, creativity, patience, determination, perseverance, and careful editing. In other words, it's real work.

With this in mind, Housel provided a list of hacks that he finds useful. Here are a few that I really relate to:

- **Marketing hack:** Make a good product that people need.
- **PR hack:** Do something newsworthy.
- **Writing hack:** Write every day for years.

> "You can't produce a baby in one month by getting nine women pregnant. It just doesn't work that way."
>
> **—WARREN BUFFETT**

- **Learning hack:** Read a book. When finished, read another.
- **Work culture hack:** Trust people and pay them well.
- **Investing hack:** Give compounding the decades it requires.
- **Savings hack:** Lower your ego and live below your means.
- **Career hack:** Work harder than is expected of you, and be nice to people.
- **Organization hack:** Clean up your mess.
- **Fundraising hack:** Make a product lots of people will pay for with decent or better margins.
- **Scale-to-a-million-users hack:** Make a product a million people need.
- **Making college more affordable hack:** Go to an in-state public school and work full time.

The takeaway is rather than focusing on what you can hack, it's a far better use of time and energy to follow tried and true principles of productivity and achievement. Here are five of my favorites:

1. **Follow the 80/20 rule:** Twenty percent of our inputs are responsible for 80 percent of our outcomes. Therefore, it would stand to reason that the ultimate hack is to identify and spend time on what has the potential to provide the greatest outcome. The rest is a distraction.

2. **Separate urgent from important:** One of the most important productivity concepts that goal-oriented individuals understand is the difference between those things that are urgent and those things that are important.

3. **Give consistent effort and have patience:** Rome wasn't built in a day. Things worth doing take time and consistent effort toward the goal.

4. **Create a stop-doing list:** To do more of the right things, you need to also stop doing the wrong ones.

5. Last but not least, **if you do something, do it well!**

History is a great teacher, showing us time and again that qualities such as focus, patience, practice, and a commitment to excellence will always trump a hack in the long run.

Saying No

I've struggled to say no to others for most of my professional life. I've worried about coming off as unapproachable or, worse, that others will think I perceive myself as being more important than them in some way. Then, I listened to an episode of *The Tim Ferriss Show* titled "How to Say No." When I tested out some of Ferriss's recommendations, I came to realize that I am actually happier and more productive when I say no to others and commit to less. Here are three strategies that have helped me get better at saying no.

Give Up the Guilt

When you begin to feel guilty for saying no to another person's request, be it for a few minutes of your time, a financial contribution, or help with a time-consuming project, it's important to weigh it against the other commitments you have already made that need your full focus.

If you're able to do both and your priorities are aligned, great. However, if saying yes to the request will mean time and attention away from something meaningful that you've already committed to, then saying no is the right thing to do.

> "Your obligation is to the highest point of contribution you can make."

—GREG MCKEOWN

Know Your Core Values

I've written at length about the importance of having and living by core values. Next time you get an ask, take a moment to stop and seriously consider whether fulfilling that need speaks to your core values. Time is both precious and limited. It's essential to choose your commitments carefully and ensure they will move you toward what is most important to you. Someone else's passion or priorities may not be your own, and that's okay.

Leverage Templates

When you decide to say no, how you choose to respond can make all the difference. In his podcast episode, Ferriss highlighted the similarities in the rejections he received when he asked successful people to contribute to one of his books. Turns out there are some common denominators of a "good" rejection, including:

- A personal acknowledgment of the individual making the request.
- An admission of your own need to focus on other priorities given previous commitments.

Saying No

- A clear statement that you cannot help in this matter.
- A note explaining that you are responding consistently in this way to all requests of this kind.

I've found that people who get a lot of requests tend to have a lot of templates. They might have one for declining speaking engagements, another for declining a podcast appearance, one for saying no to a meeting, etc. Each time you field a new type of request, consider taking an extra minute to turn your response into a template. This can make it easier to say no respectfully and thoughtfully to similar future requests.

There's great value in learning how to set limits without guilt. In the end, you might discover that saying no is the best way to say yes to something that will enable you to make your biggest contribution.

68

BS of Busy

There's a response to a commonly asked question that's become a conversational crutch: "How's it going?" "Good! Just busy."

This exchange is ubiquitous in both our personal and professional lives. It's as if busyness carries a certain status symbol. Yet being "busy" doesn't make us happier, and it doesn't make us more productive. It just means we are filling all of our available time.

Years ago, in one of our quarterly off-site meetings, a leadership team member told our facilitator, "I just don't have enough time!" The facilitator looked at her, then at all of us, and said, "As a leader, 'not enough time' is an excuse you all must take out of your vocabulary. If you are waiting for all this free time to come, it's never going to happen. It's about what you prioritize and how you use your time. Effective leaders know how to prioritize what's most important."

His words have stuck with me. Even though I still find the phrasing "I've been busy!" on the tip of my tongue when someone asks me how I've been, I make a conscious effort not to say it. I try and remind my team to do the same.

Instead of hopelessly waiting to be given the gift of more free time, consider what high achievers do to stay focused and accomplish large, long-term goals.

> "The cost of a thing is the amount of what I will call life which is required to be exchanged for it, immediately or in the long run."
>
> **—HENRY DAVID THOREAU**

They:

- Accept that time is a precious and fixed resource
- Know how to separate urgent from important
- Align their top priorities with their core purpose and/or core values
- Don't book 100 percent of their time; they value rest and relaxation
- Constantly look for things that they should stop doing
- Are selective about the people they give their energy to

When an important task isn't getting done, it's important to acknowledge and admit that you have chosen to spend your time on less important tasks (i.e., posting on Facebook and Instagram). Instead of saying, "I didn't have enough time," try saying "I chose to do X today instead of Y" or "I'm getting distracted" or "I'm focusing on the wrong things." This honesty and accountability will help you use your time more wisely, accomplish more, and be less "busy."

Goals and Standards

Goals are something you hope to achieve. Standards are uncompromising.

This was the essence of a talk I saw given by Eric Kapitulik to a group of local CEOs. Eric is the founder of The Program, an innovative leadership development firm with military roots. He and his team work with top-performing college sports programs and private companies.

Eric's description illuminated something that I had been struggling to wrap my head around—on both a personal and professional level. He explained that when we don't meet our goals, we dust ourselves off and try again. But when we don't meet our standards, there needs to be a consequence and/or accountability.

In a business context, we need both goals and standards. Goals push the organization and individuals to reach objectives. I agree with Eric that not hitting a goal is not a reason to part ways with an employee. However, if that person continuously struggles to hit the goals set with them, then that requires a more careful look.

On the other hand, an organization needs standards and principles that are uncompromising. Failure to meet those standards on a regular basis requires accountability and action;

> "You have competition every day because you set such high standards for yourself that you have to go out every day and live up to that."
>
> **—MICHAEL JORDAN**

otherwise, the standards won't mean anything or be trusted by stakeholders. A good way to think of these is in terms of "always" and "never." For instance, an organizational standard might be, "We always respond to customers within twenty-four hours, and we never promise to do something that we know we can't." The expectations are very clear.

The same is true in our family dynamics. You may have set goals as a family, but you also need standards—expectations for how we behave with one another and contribute to the family unit that are in addition to basic responsibilities. What's more is that parents can't be afraid to set consequences when those standards aren't met. To have these standards mean something, there should be a clear association between cause and effect.

For example, when your child comes in after curfew, they should know what happens next. Otherwise, the curfew is meaningless, and you have comprised both your standard and integrity. Kids also need to be empowered to call out their parents when they feel standards aren't being met.

Finally, if we truly want to achieve personal greatness, we

must have personal standards. I once heard a serial entrepreneur share that his coach calls him each morning to see if he followed his fitness plan from the previous day. If he didn't, there are predetermined consequences, such as no alcohol or dessert that day. At a higher level, when we fail to meet the standards we have laid out for ourselves, it can call our character and integrity into question.

This week, I encourage you to think a bit more about the standards you want to establish for your team, your family, and yourself. Where you set the bar has a lot to do with how much you can stand above the crowd.

Being Excellent

I once had a reader, Daniel Gross, share a story with me about a problem he faced with his family's gas-fired heater. Because it was an older furnace, he had purchased an annual service plan through his gas supplier. His gas supplier, in turn, outsourced the service plan to another company who then contracted the actual work out to a local HVAC shop.

During the annual checkup, the technician determined that the gas control valve on Daniel's unit had a slight leak and needed to be replaced; he also suggested that the system be turned off until it was repaired. The temperature was starting to drop, and after five days of no heat and endless back and forth over the phone, the local company finally scheduled a time to come out and replace the valve (about a $400 item).

A technician came to Daniel's house with a new part. Unfortunately, it was for a different type of valve—one that was completely incompatible with his system. Before leaving— without having fixed anything—the technician asked to use the bathroom and then left without flushing the toilet.

After two more days of phone calls to the HVAC company and still no heat, Daniel was told by the company that they were declaring the furnace obsolete and unrepairable. What's more, they were voiding the service agreement.

> "How you do anything is how you do everything. Your 'character' or 'nature' just refers to how you handle all the day-to-day things in life, no matter how small."
>
> **—DEREK SIVERS**

At this point, fed up and frustrated, Daniel called his local plumber, Jason Green. Jason responded that he had the right part on his truck and could fix it the next day. Even though he was incredibly busy and booked solid, Jason showed up the next morning (Saturday, probably his day off) and got Daniel's heat back on. He also cleaned up after himself.

While Jason was working, Daniel happened to go out to his driveway where Jason's truck was parked. Not only was his truck immaculate, this famous quote was written inside the door:

"We are what we repeatedly do. Excellence, then, is not an act but a habit."

Many think about excellence as an outcome. The reality, however, is that excellence is a byproduct of the many decisions we make each day and how we choose to act in each one of those instances.

Companies are very quick to spend a lot of money on marketing to demonstrate to prospective customers how great their product or service is rather than demonstrating that with excellence day in and day out. When we choose excellence, others notice.

Physical Capacity

Physical capacity is the ability to improve our health, well-being, and physical performance. This goes beyond the obvious things like what you eat and how much you exercise. Building this capacity requires us to focus on things we take for granted like sleep, stress, and our energy.

Physical capacity is simultaneously crucial and easy to overlook. While we all know health is important, so many of us ignore our physical well-being until we get bad news from our doctors. Often by that point, things are never the same, and we wish we could turn back the clock and make changes.

I know because in 2009, I was burning the candle at both ends and had a massive panic attack. At the time, I was certain I was having a heart attack and that I was taking my last few breaths.

I collapsed to the floor in my kitchen after calling 911 and was loaded into an ambulance by paramedics.

After two days of testing, I realized I'd dodged a bullet—I

was perfectly healthy; my symptoms were incited by stress and a magnesium deficiency.

Though I was healthy, believing in that moment that I was about to die clarified for me that my health was far from guaranteed. The experience prompted me to focus on my diet, recommit to regular yoga practice, and even try running for the first time in my life.

I've heard very similar stories from other people who were as lucky as I was to get a wake-up call. For too many others, it wasn't a lesson; it was the real thing.

The fact is that while our brains drive personal and professional success, it's our bodies that do the heavy lifting to carry us to those goals. The stories in this section will explore why our physical health and our cognitive performance are inextricably linked and will motivate and encourage you to evaluate your own physical well-being.

You'll read about Sean Swarner, a two-time cancer survivor who has climbed the highest mountains on Earth despite having only one functioning lung. You'll also learn how top athletes win their championships in practice, not on the playing field; how competing with others is an asset, not a negative; and how we can improve in all facets of life by improving our physical capacity and pushing our self-imposed physical limits.

We all need to remember not to take our health for granted,

even if it seems like nothing is wrong. Remember, it's hard to do anything well if you don't have the stamina to see it through. You get one vehicle to take you through life; treat it well.

Clutch Performers

At the 2018 Winter Olympics, we saw many clutch performances by top athletes in their field. Shawn White's gold medal–winning run in the half pipe to Ester Ledecka becoming the first woman to earn two golds in different sports at a single event, many incredible athletes stepped up and delivered. And they did so on the world's biggest athletic stage.

Their performances made me reflect on what it really means to be "clutch," a term often used in sports to denote a dramatic improvement in performance under pressure or doing something awe-inspiring at the last possible moment—turning defeat into victory.

Certainly, there is a strong mental component of not caving under pressure and letting the moment overtake you. However, I'm of the belief that the biggest contributor to having a clutch performance is everything that goes on behind the scenes—well in advance of the actual performance. The countless days and hours of practice and mental preparation. The blood, sweat, and tears shed. The exhaustion. The grind.

Much like the myth of the overnight success, when we label someone's performance as clutch, we are attributing an unexplained force to their success. I see this as a form of cognitive dissonance as it allows us to relieve ourselves of the

> "When you're one of the leaders of the team, there are no days off."

—TOM BRADY

obligations and countless hours of commitment, practice, and hard work that are required for high-level success, especially when it's under pressure.

The truth is, being clutch has far more to do with what we do before stepping onto the stage or into the spotlight than being in the moment itself.

When Michael Phelps's goggles filled with water during his two-hundred-meter butterfly at the 2008 Summer Olympics, he was still able to win the gold. He had visualized the entire race and counted out his strokes well in advance of the actual race day so that even though he couldn't see, he was clear on where he was going. Clutch or preparation?

We all have the ability to be clutch performers; we just need to do the work. And as leaders, we cannot be afraid to make practice uncomfortable or more difficult than what others deem necessary.

Trough and Peak

At the age of thirteen, Sean Swarner was a happy-go-lucky eighth grader playing a baseball game when he heard a pop in his knee. The next day, all his joints were swollen. A few days after that, he was diagnosed with stage four Hodgkin's lymphoma and given a prognosis of three months to live.

He immediately began aggressive treatment, adding sixty-plus pounds to his small frame as a result of various steroids. While his friends were focused on trivial things, such as what shoes they wore and how popular they were, Swarner was focused on fighting for his life. He borrowed a visualization technique he learned from his swimming training and would imagine a microscopic spaceship flying around in his body with chemotherapy guns, killing all the cancer.

A year after his diagnosis, Swarner beat the cancer and was in remission. He refocused his efforts on being a kid and playing sports, including returning to competitive swimming.

After being in remission for twenty months, Swarner went in for one of his regular checkups. It was then that he learned that doctors had discovered a new, completely unrelated cancer in his body called Askin's tumor.

Not only was Swarner the only person in the world to have been diagnosed with both Hodgkin's disease and Askin's tumor,

> "Want to feel wealthy? Take away everything money can buy and look at what you have left."
>
> **—SEAN SWARNER**

but the latter has a 6 percent survival rate. Given just fourteen days to live, Swarner was started on treatment, the goal of which was to extend his life as long as possible. However, the chemo was so intense that he was put into a medically induced coma for each cycle, and the radiation was so severe that he lost the use of one of his lungs.

Miraculously, Swarner beat cancer again, even though he does not remember anything about being a sixteen-year-old. Understandably, he wanted to enjoy the lost years of his youth. In college, he focused on having fun and decided to become a psychology major to eventually help other cancer patients.

Then one day, he decided that to really help and make an impact, he needed to scream hope from the highest platform in the world: Mount Everest.

With only one lung, Swarner became the first cancer survivor to summit the peak. Ironically, an illness forced him to stay behind at camp on the day his group attempted the summit, which they weren't able to reach due to inclement weather. After recovering from being ill, the weather cleared, and Swarner was able to summit on his first attempt.

Since Everest, Swarner has gone on to become the world's first cancer survivor to complete the Explorer's Grand Slam—scaling the highest point on all seven continents and then hiking to the North and South Poles. On his last trip to the North Pole, he carried a massive flag with the names of thousands of people touched by cancer. The last time we connected, he shared he was preparing to run seven marathons, in seven days, in seven continents.

Incredibly, Swarner considers himself lucky. Lucky for the knee injury that likely saved his life—twice—and for the serious illness that kept him behind his group on Everest, allowing him to summit on a clear day. By choosing to focus on living rather than dying, he is an inspiration and a testament to the human spirit.

The Grind

In 2016, inspired by Brian Scudamore and Cam Herold, I wrote a Vivid Vision for our company describing what Acceleration Partners would look and feel like by January 1, 2020. It included some very ambitious goals for the organization, almost all of which we met or exceeded.

Serendipitously, in the summer of 2019, while drafting a new Vivid Vision for our company, I had the opportunity to climb the Grouse Grind, a 1.8 mile hike up Grouse Mountain in Vancouver, BC, with 2,800 feet of elevation gain and 2,830 stairs up to the summit. It's affectionately called "Mother Nature's Stairmaster" and is a mental and physical exercise in resilience.

As I made the climb, I came to appreciate that the Grouse Grind trail is a powerful metaphor for any difficult challenge. Each quarter of the ascent mirrored aspects of our company's Vivid Vision journey.

The First Quarter
When we started up Grouse Mountain, we had a lot of energy and optimism. The reality of what lay ahead had not yet sunk in. As a result, our pace was probably faster than it should have been at the outset. I also drank far too much of my water too early. In retrospect, this reminded me how important it is to pace

|| "The best view comes after the hardest climb."

—ANONYMOUS

yourself and conserve energy when faced with a long, challenging experience as you may need to tap into those reserves when the going really gets tough. If your journey is going better than expected once you get past the halfway point, that's the time to turn up the pace.

Halfway Point

Similar to many endeavors, the halfway point is a great time for reflection and assessment about how you're feeling and what your supply situation is looking like. It can also be a time to mentally readjust to get through the remainder of the climb based on the reality of the first half. In our case, we realized that reaching the time goal we'd set for ourselves wouldn't be possible. So we set a new one.

Third Quarter

In relation to both our climb and AP's path to reaching our 2020 Vivid Vision, the third-quarter portion of the journey typically comprises the greatest challenges. On Grouse Mountain, the third-quarter section was the steepest part of the climb. Fatigue set in, and I became too focused on each step; I lost perspective of the fact that we were 75 percent of the way to the summit. This same phenomenon often presents itself in one's business, especially when progress goals are high.

The Summit

There are numerous studies on the burst of energy that people get in the last leg of a race or upon seeing the finish line. I certainly experienced this on my hike. Even though I was exhausted, as soon as the summit came into view, I began to sprint. The desire to reach the goal overrode how my body felt.

This made me realize that the most dangerous part of a difficult endeavor is the point in between the three-quarter mark and the finish; when you are mentally or physically exhausted but don't yet have the top of the summit in sight.

Upon reaching the summit, I made a video for my team to remind them that the finish line for our Vivid Vision was only a few quarters away.

My advice for both a tough climb and a big goal is this:

Start slower than you think you need to. Reassess and adjust halfway to your goal. When you reach the three-quarters point, remember to look forward. Last, but not least, make sure to keep that finish line in sight.

Breaking Barriers

Barriers are meant to be broken, even when doing so seems unachievable. Nowhere is this truer than in running. The first major running barrier was broken by Roger Bannister, who, on May 6, 1954, busted through the four-minute-mile barrier with a time of three minutes, fifty-nine and four-tenths of a second. In doing this, he accomplished a feat that many had previously thought was impossible.

Then, curiously, numerous other runners broke the four-minute barrier over the next few years. Presumably they were aided by improvements in training, coaching, and technology, but psychology also played a big part: these other runners now knew it could be done. Today, an elite high school runner can be expected to accomplish this feat.

Oregon runner Justin Gallegos has recently gained national attention for his goal to break a barrier and run a half marathon in less than two hours. Oregon is the alma mater of Nike founder Phil Knight and a training ground for elite runners. However, two hours for a half marathon certainly doesn't sound elite... what's missing?

Justin Gallegos has cerebral palsy. For him, running is both a joy and a physical struggle.

As a toddler and preschooler, Gallegos used a walker and

> "I was once a kid in leg braces who could barely put [one] foot in front of the other! Now I have signed a contract with Nike Running!"
>
> **—JUSTIN GALLEGOS**

did physical therapy to improve his gait, according to *Canadian Running Magazine.* He then began competing in long-distance running in high school and caught the attention of Nike. He also helped Nike develop a shoe designed for runners with disabilities.

Justin made history by becoming the first professional athlete with cerebral palsy to be signed by Nike. Nike surprised him with a contract offer by sending a video crew to capture the event at one of his practices, a video he believed was for a World Cerebral Palsy Day promotion. At the end of a run, a director from Nike presented Justin with the contract. He was moved to tears, as are most people who watch the video of the event.

Justin's courage and determination for a half marathon under two hours will inspire a whole group of athletes and humans in a variety of different but important ways. I, for one, have committed to run my first half marathon by next summer.

Character Coach

I have a love-hate relationship with youth sports today. I think sports are great for kids; they get exercise and learn the values of being part of a team, hard work, practice, and competition, and they also learn the discomfort of trying something new.

My issue is with the parents. From my perspective, too many parents have gone from being spirited spectators to being overly—and sometimes viciously—invested in their children's athletic endeavors and achievements. This includes aggressively coaching from the sidelines during the game and antagonistically engaging with referees (many of whom are kids) and other parents.

All this behavior does is create a fear of failure.

Somewhere along the way, a child's individual success in athletics has become a more relevant benchmark of parental success. What happened to honoring kids who are great team players with good character?

To be clear, I have no issue with parents investing time and energy in coaching their kids in athletics. I would hope, however, that those same parents would put as much or greater weight into coaching character. Sadly, what I've seen firsthand is conduct contrary to this aspiration. For example, with parents who openly disrespect a referee, 99 percent of the time, you'll see that their kids do the same.

> "We live in a culture that teaches us to promote and advertise ourselves and to master the skills required for success, but that gives little encouragement to humility, sympathy, and honest self-confrontation, which are necessary for building character."
>
> **—DAVID BROOKS**

Data from the National Collegiate Athletic Association (NCAA) in the United States shows that about 5 percent of kids who play high school sports will go on to play sports in college. And less than 1 percent of those will have a career in professional sports. In other words, 99 percent of children will be done with organized sports when they graduate college.

Conversely,

- 100 percent of children will be part of a team at some point in their adult life and career.
- 100 percent will face a disappointment that requires resilience and poise.
- 100 percent will need to learn to work with someone they disagree with and/or dislike.
- 100 percent will have the ability to impact others with kindness or generosity.
- 100 percent will be humbled or need to show humility.

- 100 percent will have a challenging situation with a peer or friend.

The coaching kids will need for success both in athletics and in life focuses on preparing for these inevitabilities. If you are a parent, coach, or educator and you truly want long-term success for your kids or anyone you lead, then my recommendation is to focus on imparting character instead of on attaining momentary results.

While it's always great to hear accolades about my kids' performance on the field, as their parent, I'd much rather have someone tell me unsolicited they are a "good kid" or hear that one of my kids showed incredible sportsmanship or how they selflessly helped a peer. Those are skills that will take them further in life.

Peloton Principle

I am a huge fan of my Peloton bike and have been incredibly impressed at the company's amazing growth over the past few years. The cofounder and CEO of Peloton, John Foley, attributes the company's success to its two core philosophies: "don't let perfect be the enemy of good" and "the avalanche starts with the pebble."

The word *peloton* comes from road bicycle racing and is derived from the French word for "ball." As many of us have seen when watching the Tour de France, the peloton is the group of riders who ride/partner together in a formation.

In this formation, riders who are positioned up front allow for those riders in the middle of the formation to draft, thus reducing their drag (effort) by as much as 40 percent. The peloton rotates throughout the journey, giving everyone in the group the opportunity to take turns pushing and resting. This concept is actually modeled after the formation of a flock of birds that fly in the same way.

The peloton is a successful strategy as it allows each team member to perform at their best while also efficiently conserving energy. Teams also often use this strategy to help support and protect the rider who has the strongest chance of winning the race.

> "Individual commitment to a group effort—that is what makes a team work, a company work, a society work, a civilization work."
>
> **—VINCE LOMBARDI**

The concept of a peloton is also an instructive metaphor for those times in our personal and professional lives when we need to step up to the front and take the headwind for others, allowing them to catch up and perform better over the long haul.

At the same time, it's not possible or a good use of a rider's energy to stay at the head of the pack for too long. What's needed is self-awareness for when we need to fall back, regain our energy, and let others take the lead.

As their core philosophies reflect, Peloton's success has come by making steady progress each day. This serves as a good reminder that achieving success and reaching our goals requires that we continue moving forward while also being mindful about how we're performing along the way and being aware when we need to step forward or drop back.

Environmental Effect

We all want to believe that we have the willpower to consistently make good decisions and develop good habits. As it turns out though, research shows that willpower is a limited resource; the more we tap into it, the less we have in reserves. Because your willpower bucket tends to be at its height early in the day, this is also one of the reasons to get started on the right foot with a healthy, productive morning routine.

When it comes to pursuing goals, what often matters more than discipline and willpower is the environment and people we surround ourselves with on a regular basis.

I think it's helpful to examine this concept of environment from two perspectives: micro and macro.

Micro Environment

Want to watch less TV? Take the batteries out of the remote and put it across the room.

Want to run more in the morning? Put your shoes next to your bed and go to sleep in your running clothes.

Want to eat less? Use smaller utensils and dishware.

The author of the research-based book *Mindless Eating* found that, "If you use a big spoon, you'll eat more. If you serve yourself on a big plate, you'll eat more. If you move the small

> "There's just one way to radically change your behavior: radically change your environment."
>
> **—BJ FOGG**

bowl of chocolates on your desk six feet away from you, you'll eat half as much."

These small changes can significantly affect your micro environment and allow you to reserve willpower so that you can tap into it when you need it for bigger decisions.

Macro Environment

Controlling our macro environment is harder and can involve some tough choices, from where we choose to live to whom we choose to spend our time with. As Jim Rohn said, "We are the average of the five people we spend the most time with."

The "whom we associate with" aspect can often be the most difficult for people. But the reality is, if you want to drink less and your close friends go to the bar four nights a week, it's probably in your best interest to find new friends to hang out with the majority of the time.

Rather than deplete your willpower by joining them at the bar and hoping to not be enticed to drink, the easier path would be to join them one night a week and then fill your other nights with friends and activities that don't involve alcohol.

Same thing if you want to be in a happy, loyal marriage. Hanging around others who are unfaithful in their relationship or spending time in environments where this behavior is condoned or encouraged is probably not the best choice for this objective.

In summary, to accomplish what you want most, it's important to think carefully and intentionally on a macro level about how to associate with people and environments (including companies) that support your objectives. This may also mean removing yourself from those that do not.

On a micro level, think about how and where you can decrease the friction for things you want to do and accomplish and increase friction for those that aren't in alignment with those goals.

True Team Sacrifice

I have seen a lot of gutsy sports performances in my life, but twenty-five-year-old German gymnast Andreas Toba's feat in the 2016 Summer Olympic event may have topped them all.

In his individual floor routine, Toba landed awkwardly on his knee and cried out in agony before collapsing to the mat. He was unable to finish because of what was eventually diagnosed as a torn ACL. He sat in tears on the sidelines with his teammates, knowing his individual chances for an Olympic medal were finished.

However, Toba realized that Germany needed him to complete his final routine on the pommel horse for the team to have a chance to advance. So he limped out in visible pain and gutted through a performance on the pommel horse, which required an aerial dismount. In doing so, he secured Germany's qualification with the very last spot in the medal round and demonstrated what it means to make a true sacrifice for your team.

I am in awe of Toba's incredible and selfless act and hope that we could each make a similar sacrifice if called upon to lift up one of our teammates or to reach our common goals.

> "I am a member of a team, and I rely on the team, I defer to it and sacrifice for it, because the team, not the individual, is the ultimate champion."   **—MIA HAMM**

Two Hours

Most of us waste two hours on a Saturday morning without realizing where the time went. For Eliud Kipchoge, two hours changed his life.

On Saturday, October 12, 2019, Kipchoge, a world champion runner from Kenya, became the first man to run a marathon in under two hours. On a specially chosen course, Kipchoge clocked one hour, fifty-nine minutes, 40.2 seconds.

Until recently, running a sub-two-hour marathon was a feat many believed impossible. This led Nike to launch Breaking2 in 2014, a project with the sole purpose of creating a team of elite runners focused on breaking the two-hour-marathon barrier.

Kipchoge was one of those runners.

Reverse engineering the vision is where history separates the big doers from the big dreamers. Having a big idea or a vision is commendable, but it won't get you very far. What's required to make that vision a reality are resources, planning, and action. This is what Nike did with Breaking2, bringing together a world-class team of athletes, scientists, and product designers.

In addition to vision, nothing was left to chance for this historic sub-two-hour marathon attempt.

On the day of the run, Kipchoge was supported by forty-one professional runners who acted as pacesetters. Running in an

|| "A goal without a plan is just a wish."

—ANONYMOUS

aerodynamic V shape to shield wind, they each followed a pace car that projected the ideal position on the road with a laser beam.

Even the location of the race was chosen with great plan and preparation. It was flat, the temperature was perfect for running this time of year, it was close to sea level, and it was located only one time zone away from Kipchoge's training camp in Kenya. In 2017, Nike had held a well-publicized event with three runners, including Kipchoge, in the first attempt at breaking the two-hour barrier. No runner succeeded. Subsequent attempts also failed. However, instead of giving up, the team focused on learning from each situation. They reevaluated, reassessed, and readjusted. Those lessons helped make Kipchoge's sub-two-hour marathon a reality.

There are many people who let self-limiting beliefs get in the way of them doing things they never thought possible. Similarly, there are dreamers who sit frustrated, watching other people do what they had conceived but never acted upon. New breakthroughs need big thinkers but also discipline, planning, and execution to bring them to fruition.

Kipchoge's accomplishment reminds me of the motto I have developed for my kids: "You can have anything you desire as long as you are willing to do what's required."

Color War

One of my favorite activities as a kid was a game called Color War. Color War is a one-hundred-year-old tradition that started at sleepover camps and is organized in the spirit of the Olympics.

The camp divides into two colors for either a few days or weeks of competition, and campers in each age group are asked to take leadership roles. It's not just athletics; there is often singing, bunk bed–making inspections, military-style lineups, and even silent meals that are judged for points. It can be intense.

For several days, your best friends are your competitors, and both level of effort and discipline are raised significantly. But then suddenly, it's over, and there are celebrations and tears and everything returns to normal.

I loved Color War and never ran harder, stayed quieter when asked, or had a tidier bed than during those summers. As my kids now participate in Color War, it has allowed me to reflect on what it taught me about leadership and competing in life.

I strongly believe many of today's parents and schools are doing a disservice to a whole generation by trying to eliminate, discourage, or pretend that competition does not exist. Instead, they offer trophies, praise, and other awards in exchange for often minimal effort or basic participation. In doing this, we are ignoring some of the principal benefits of competition:

> "The will to win, the desire to succeed, the urge to reach your full potential...these are the keys that will unlock the door to personal excellence."
>
> **—ANONYMOUS**

1. Bringing out one's individual best
2. Learning how to be a humble winner and a resilient loser
3. Discipline and persistence

At every stage of life, we will win some, and we will lose some. But without the right preparation, we won't do either well.

Through healthy competition, we're given opportunities to reach our best and fullest potential—and bring them out in others as well. The word "compete" even comes from the Latin root meaning "strive together." It is a foundation of excellence.

This desire to elevate individual and team performance collectively is the real goal of competition and something that we should be encouraging more in our personal and professional lives.

Good Sportsmanship

As seen in Color War, competition is a vital part of achievement and elevated performance. But even though there are many examples of the value of competition, this concept is still often misunderstood and underappreciated.

The reality is that we regularly compete in most aspects of our lives. We compete for jobs we want, college admission spots, and new clients and employees. However, this doesn't mean we should abandon having character.

One of my favorite examples of competition and character comes from high school baseball. In 2018, Minnesota high school pitcher Ty Koehn faced his best friend, Jack Kocon, in the sectional championship game. Koehn struck out Kocon to earn the final out and advance Koehn's team to the state tournament.

As his team rushed to the pitcher's mound to celebrate, Koehn immediately headed to home plate and gave Kocon a big hug before joining his teammates in celebration.

When asked about his reaction, Koehn said that he wanted his friend to know their friendship was more important than the outcome of the game.

The scene reminded me of a video I saw a few years back of a softball player named Sara Tucholsky. Tucholsky had hit a three-run home run, the first in her college career, but she had missed

> "The key difference between winners and losers is how they win and lose."
>
> **—ANONYMOUS**

making contact with first base on her first go-round. As she ran back to tag first base, she tore her ACL.

As per official rules, none of Tucholsky's teammates could assist her in running the bases, which she couldn't do because of her injured knee. The umpires also pointed out that Tucholsky's hit would only count as a two-run single if she were replaced by a pinch runner.

What happened next was one of the most incredible acts of sportsmanship ever seen: Tucholsky's opponents lifted her up and carried her around the bases, briefly placing her to tag each one. This act cost their team the victory.

Competing is about elevating our own game. It's about practicing, getting better, and having the will to win as a team. Instead of winning at all costs or wishing failure on others, real winners always prioritize character over winning itself. True sportsmanship requires that we know how to win well and be gracious in defeat.

Tri It

In 2017, I completed my first Olympic triathlon—a long-term goal of mine. During the triathlon, I reflected on the lessons I had learned from the training process and came up with eight that I wanted to share:

1. **Importance of delayed gratification:** If you want to develop the discipline of a world-class performer, there is no better way than by picking a goal that only takes a short time to execute but months of daily discipline.

2. **The best goals are ones that scare you:** Last year, I resolved to pick at least one annual goal that terrifies me, at least a little. The idea is to force myself out of my comfort zone (mental or physical) and be emboldened by what I didn't think I could do.

3. **Pick a date:** The year before, I set the same goal to complete a triathlon. The difference is that I never picked a specific date/event. Then, I got injured and had a bunch of other convenient excuses. This year, as soon as I found an event I was interested in, I picked the date and paid the entrance fee.

4. **The value of a coach/mentor:** In preparation for my first triathlon, I worked with a great coach who designed a training plan for me and was my weekly accountability partner.

> "Happiness does not come from doing easy work but from the afterglow of satisfaction that comes after the achievement of a difficult task that demanded our best."
>
> **—THEODORE ISAAC RUBIN**

5. **Focus on what works for you, not what others are doing:** When it comes to swimming, my strong suit is the breaststroke. However, for a triathlon, most agree that the front crawl is more appropriate, so that was what I trained for. On race day, I started out my swim with this technique, but about five minutes in, I abandoned it for the breaststroke. Right away, it made things easier. In retrospect, I may have done even better during my swim component had I not cared what anyone thought and trained for the breaststroke from the start.

6. **Alternate your horizon:** There were times during my training and the actual race when it was motivational to look ahead and think about the finish line. Other times, it was better for me to just look down and focus on taking one step at a time. Both motivate you in different ways.

7. **Practice on stage:** My coach suggested that I practice on the actual course, which I had delayed because of my travel schedule. When I did test the swim two days before the event, I realized that swimming in open water (versus in a

pool) made me nauseous. If I hadn't trained on the actual course for my swim, I wouldn't have had the time to make adjustments and would have been in trouble on race day.

8. **Start what you finish:** In her bestselling book *Grit*, author Angela Duckworth talks about her family's rule of "finishing what you start," be it a season of sports, instrument lessons, etc. The idea is that while you don't have to do it again, you cannot quit once you have started.

Whatever your goal, if it doesn't scare you a bit, it's probably not really a stretch for you.

Putting Yourself First

Many of us don't prioritize our own life goals and needs. We put ourselves last and too often say yes to other things and people, which divides our energy into too many disparate activities. The result is that we aren't as successful, nor are we as effective at helping others as we could be.

There seems to be a lot of confusion around the concept of putting one's self first in relation to being selfish. I don't see them as one in the same. Being selfish is more about believing that the world revolves around you and your needs and not caring about the well-being of others; putting yourself first is about not compromising your own needs.

If we don't put ourselves first, then everyone we come across tends to get a suboptimal version of us. To be at our best—for ourselves and others—we need to make sure we are living in a way that leaves us happy, healthy, and rested. Some of the most generous and giving people I know are those who are very disciplined about their own priorities and goals. The result is they have the capacity to give the most in a sustained way.

Here are three simple tips to help you get better about putting yourself first:

1. **Say no:** If we say yes to everything everyone asks us to do, we

> "Remember always that you not only have the right to be
> an individual, you have an obligation to be one."
>
> **—ELEANOR ROOSEVELT**

will never be in control of our own priorities. Author Derek Sivers addresses this with what he calls the "hell yeah or no" test. Simply put, if you aren't jumping with joy to do it, you should just say no and relieve yourself of the associated guilt.

2. **Prioritize basic needs:** Sleeping, eating, and movement (exercise) are all basic needs that should be an uncompromising priority in our lives. To point number one, this often requires saying no to other things.

3. **Keep a journal:** I keep coming across article after article about the benefits of journaling. An interesting aspect of this practice is that it provides a window into your stream of consciousness, self-accountability, and mindfulness.

The next time you find yourself making an excuse for something that you want to do for yourself, I encourage you to take a step back and consider the three tips provided above. If you are constantly putting your own needs and goals behind those of others, you'll likely end up being too tired or resentful to enjoy your own success and achievement. Putting yourself first isn't selfish; it's often the best thing you can do in the service of others.

Emotional Capacity

Emotional capacity measures your ability to overcome limiting beliefs, your ease in adapting to challenging situations, and the quality of your relationships. No matter how talented, driven, or energized you are, you cannot achieve your goals if your emotional capacity is low.

A common mistake people make is assuming emotional characteristics are a fixed part of their personality. Just as we can grow intellectually by learning or improve physically by exercising, we can get better at managing our emotional reactions and keeping ourselves steady when inevitable adversity strikes.

None of us exist in a vacuum, and as you grow, you'll need to change your relationship with the environment you're in and the people you're surrounded by.

Often, our own self-limiting beliefs are our greatest obstacle to improving our emotional capacity. Many of us are tempted to take the easy way out and make environmental excuses to avoid pursuing difficult goals. If you've told yourself that you don't have time to write a book or that you're too old to start regularly exercising, you're probably selling yourself short or are afraid to try.

It can be difficult to accept that we are actually in control of most of what happens to us. For whatever reason, that reality provides more discomfort than confidence to many.

We each have a responsibility to help others overcome their own self-limiting beliefs. This is one of the key themes of Friday Forward—when you read stories of people who overcame challenging circumstances to accomplish meaningful goals, it reinforces the idea that each of us can achieve more than we expect. When we push aside our self-imposed limits, we help others do the same.

Another core component of emotional capacity is the quality of our relationships. Even the most self-reliant people—and I include myself in that category—are shaped every day by the people closest to us. It is important to build relationships with people who help you grow and pull back from relationships that drain you of your energy.

The stories in this section go into detail on all these topics: building relationships that matter, showing gratitude to others, learning from failure, and focusing on what you can control rather than worrying on what you can't. You'll read the story of Michael Weisser, a rabbi who was targeted by a Ku Klux Klan leader and responded with grace and kindness. You'll learn about Mary-Claire King, who reacted to the worst week of her life by delivering a grant presentation that led to a groundbreaking cancer research study that has likely saved millions of lives. You'll understand what energy vampires are and how they keep you from reaching your full potential.

These stories will push you to reconsider your relationship to the world around you. Ask yourself: what limiting beliefs are you struggling to overcome? What challenges have you encountered where a different emotional reaction would've made a difference? What relationships in your life do you need to invest more time in—and which ones aren't worth the effort?

We can occasionally be our own worst enemy. Building emotional capacity will help you avoid that stumbling block.

Energy Vampires

I've written before about the importance of engaging more deliberately with people who provide positive energy and help build your capacity to elevate. But it's also important to examine people at the opposite end of the spectrum: energy vampires.

As monk-turned-business consultant Dandapani explains, we all have a finite amount of energy to use each day, and we're exposed to people who either fill us with energy or drain us of energy. People who drain our energy are known as energy vampires. These people could be colleagues, friends, family members—even people we encounter while out running errands.

Dandapani suggests that one of the first things to do when dealing with these people is to figure out whether they are a temporary vampire or they are inherently an energy vampire. Temporary energy vampires might be going through a difficult time in their lives (divorce, loss of a family member or job, etc.). In the short term, they need to lean on others, and that's okay, even though it may be draining.

Conversely, inherent energy vampires are always this way, and they aren't looking to change. The easiest way to identify this type of person is to assess how you feel after you walk away

> "I have only so much energy in the day and I want to invest it. I want to invest it into the people that I love, the people that are investing back in me."
>
> **—DANDAPANI**

from them. If you feel exhausted, then chances are that person is an energy vampire.

Here are some common characteristics of energy vampires:

- **The victim or blamer:** They consistently talk about how they are always getting the short end of the stick in life. They find external blame wherever possible and like to make others feel guilty.
- **The center of attention:** They always seem to make themselves the center of attention in any room or conversation; they like to stand out.
- **The narcissist:** They are consumed with themselves and their own problems; they take very little time to think about others or how to make their lives better.
- **The drama queen/king:** They love the highs and lows, are surrounded by drama constantly, and want to bring everyone along for the ride.

While the best solution is to avoid these people altogether, it can be challenging if they are your coworkers, close friends, or even family members. And when we try to move away from them, we often feel guilty about it.

However difficult, it's essential that you find a way to break free. What you're doing is looking after yourself and protecting your energy. When you allow an energy vampire to drain you, they are depleting your ability to help and uplift others and be the best version of yourself.

It's not about being confrontational; it's about learning to tactfully avoid energy vampires and, if that's not possible, then learning how to not engage with them. Your energy is best used elsewhere.

With Gratitude

A few years back, my family and I started implementing a practice that was recommended to me by a mentor of mine, Warren Rustand. His advice was, after your stay at a hotel had come to an end, leave a handwritten note thanking the person who cleaned your room along with a monetary tip.

There are many reasons why this is a good thing to do, but three in particular are:

1. It's an act of gratitude. Practicing gratitude has numerous benefits for our health and state of mind.
2. It shows respect, dignity, and appreciation for someone's hard work, work that often goes unnoticed.
3. The tip is often insignificant to you but meaningful to them.

A friend of mine was also inspired by Warren's advice and had begun leaving a tip with a thank-you note after his hotel stays. He shared that after a recent stay at an Airbnb in Guatemala, he'd left a fifteen-dollar tip each day to the person who had cooked and cleaned for them. To his surprise, he received a note from the owner a few days later that read:

"I want to thank you so much for being so generous with Sandra's tips. She told me today she was able to take her child

> "Gratitude can transform common days into thanksgivings, turn routine jobs into joy, and change ordinary opportunities into blessings."
>
> **—WILLIAM ARTHUR WARD**

to the dentist and to deparasite her other child from amoebas. It really made a difference; thanks for your generosity."

In our haste, we often neglect to show appreciation for the little things or take the time to thank and acknowledge those who have served us. And the reality is, these individuals are likely far less fortunate.

We're all guilty of focusing on our first world problems and overlooking the challenges/circumstances of others. When we take the time to think about and recognize those who have served us in some way, with nothing to gain from doing so, it has a positive impact that is greater than we can imagine. I also believe it's simply good karma. I encourage you to take the time to sincerely thank someone who's done something to serve you and see if you can improve their life in some small way. It'll very likely make a difference to them and, as a bonus, it'll also likely make you feel good about yourself.

A relatively small gesture can make a real difference in the life of another person.

Choice Words

Something I have learned, both as a parent and in my own leadership journey, is the importance of the words we use, especially when we give praise or critical feedback. When we critique, the inclination is often to attack the recipient personally rather than address the problematic behavior they are exhibiting.

For example, I have encountered many managers who may think a team member is not a strong strategic thinker. The common approach is to tell the person that they "need to be more strategic," which is rarely received well. This approach makes the person think their personality is being criticized rather than their actions.

A more effective strategy is to discuss the specific outcome in question. In the case above, a manager might review an example of a project deliverable that was too tactical and show how the employee could have been more strategic in their assessment.

While subtle, there's a significant difference between telling someone they are "not strategic" versus telling them they are not demonstrating the strategic thinking the work requires. While many of us believe our character traits are fixed, it is easier for us to commit to changing our behavior.

Sometimes people even criticize in a deeply hurtful way. Recently, in response to my articles and speeches on company

> "People evolve, and so your relationships must evolve with them. Care personally; don't put people in boxes and leave them there."
>
> **—KIM SCOTT**

culture, people shared with me that past leaders regularly told them they weren't smart enough, didn't understand people, weren't management material, and made other types of personal attacks.

Sometimes we must have difficult conversations. However, character attacks don't actually help people improve. If anything, they can have the opposite effect; I've had people tell me that receiving this type of personal criticism damaged their confidence for years.

This same principle also applies to parenting. There is a significant difference between calling a child stupid versus noting that they did something that was not smart—or between calling a child lazy rather than telling them they are acting lazy.

Conversely but similarly, I once heard a well-respected child psychologist share that we should praise children for their behavior, not characteristics. For example, instead of telling a child they "are smart," it's better to tell them something they did that was smart. In this way, you are focusing on their behavior rather than ascribing a character trait they don't control.

Feedback isn't always easy to give or receive. However, how we give that feedback—the words and tone of voice we use—can make all the difference in the world.

This week, think about feedback you need to give to someone or even yourself. Pay attention to your word choice, tone, inflection, and what you're really trying to convey before it's given. That intentional thought can greatly impact how it is received.

Love and Hate

In 1991, Michael Weisser, along with his wife, Julie, and three of their five children, moved from New York City to Lincoln, Nebraska, for Weisser's new position: cantor and spiritual leader of South Street Temple.

As they were moving in and unpacking, the phone rang. When they answered, the caller said, "You're going to be sorry you moved in, Jew boy," and then hung up.

A few days later, the Weissers received a package in the mail containing hateful anti-Semitic and racist materials along with a business card from the Ku Klux Klan that read, "The KKK is watching you scum." The police suggested that the caller and antagonist was very likely Larry Trapp, the local Grand Dragon of the White Knights of the KKK chapter in Nebraska. Trapp, as it happens, was also a double amputee, having lost his legs to advanced diabetes at a young age.

Weisser was worried for his family but decided to take a different approach. He got Trapp's phone number from a friend and began leaving messages on his answering machine, such as, *"Larry, there's a lot of love out there. You're not getting any of it. Don't you want some?"* *"Larry, you'd better think about all this hatred that you are involved in because you're going to have to deal with God one day."*

|| "The truth is, human nature is good, not bad."

—RABBI MICHAEL WEISSER

This turned into a regular monthly routine, with Weisser calling and leaving a message for Trapp at 3:00 p.m. every Thursday. One Thursday, Trapp answered the call by screaming profanities and asking Weisser what he wanted. Weisser replied that he knew Trapp was disabled and offered to give him a ride to the grocery store, to which Trapp responded that he was all set and told him not to call anymore.

He kept calling and leaving messages of love. Then, one day, Weisser's phone rang. It was Trapp, who asked, "Is this the rabbi?" When Weisser affirmed that it was, Trapp responded by saying, "I want to get out of what I am doing, and I don't know how."

Despite warnings from his family, Weisser decided to visit Trapp at his house that night to "break bread." After talking for hours, Weisser learned of the severe emotional and physical abuse Trapp had suffered at the hands of his father. As a child, he would often hide for hours to avoid a beating. It became clear to Weisser that Trapp's hateful actions were a manifestation of having never felt loved.

Over the next year, Trapp became a fixture in the community, making amends and talking to groups about the perils of hatred. Around this time, his health also began to deteriorate.

Surprising everyone, the Weissers invited Trapp to come live with them, an offer he accepted. Trapp stayed with them until his death a year later. During this time, he also converted to Judaism. The day of his funeral, the synagogue was packed with people who would have never expected to be there just a few years before.

I have many takeaways from this story, but here are a few that stand out the most:

- When we put hate out into the world, we get hate in return. This cycle continues until someone is willing to break it. This pattern of behavior is sadly becoming prevalent across the world today.
- In all aspects of our lives, we can all be better at seeking to understand. What we see on the surface is often the symptom, not the cause.
- It takes an enlightened person to get to the why behind people's actions, decisions, behaviors, and beliefs that otherwise seem inexcusable.

Rose, Thorn, and Bud

Across most family dinner tables, parents often pose the question, "How was your day?" Unfortunately, this is usually followed by the truncated response, "Fine," resulting in awkward dead air.

Although commonplace, these types of interactions can be improved by changing the approach. For example, a few years ago, I was invited to a business colleague's house for dinner. Their family practice was for each member to talk about the best part of their day, the worst part of their day, and then something they were grateful for.

I was struck by the quality and thoughtfulness of the discussion, so much so that we decided to adopt a similar discussion format in our family that we call "rose, thorn, bud." We each talk about the best part of our day (the rose), the worst part of our day (thorn), and then note something that we are looking forward to (bud). The kids really enjoy it and are often the ones who prompt us to start the conversation, and we get much better stories about what's happening in their lives.

Posing these types of questions is aligned with the Socratic method, a powerful teaching tactic used by many business and law schools. It's founded on the belief that asking thought-provoking questions will stimulate critical thinking, draw out ideas, and expose underlying presumptions.

|| "The unexamined life is not worth living."

—SOCRATES

Asking good questions will help our team grow by teaching us to think about problems differently and offer better solutions. We can all work on improving the types of questions we ask in our regular interactions with clients and one another rather than jumping to offer advice and answers. Two questions in particular that I like to ask when doing my one-on-ones with my employees are (1) what's working and (2) what's not working. The latter question tends to produce especially good insights.

Having Doubt

I always enjoy when I have a chance to sit down with my good friend Conor Neill, a well-respected scholar and coach on the subject of public speaking. Conor has helped many people drastically improve their public speaking abilities by teaching them how to develop a confident, compelling message, leaving their listener with no doubt that they are an expert in their subject matter.

A recent discussion between us quickly turned to the growing entrenchment in rigid ideology around the world. Conor connected this to the concept of faith and shared a story about a devoutly religious friend of his who was open to all questions and criticism about his beliefs.

This friend spoke with Conor about the importance of having faith in the face of doubt. His premise is that if you have only doubt, you're cynical. On the flip side, if you do not doubt, then your beliefs begin to border on fanaticism in the most extreme cases.

This is a powerful concept and, in many ways, explains the dynamics undermining the very divided political environment in the United States and around the world. Today, people seem less open to dialogue and respectful debate or even trying to understand an alternate perspective. Instead, they're defaulting to rigid ideology or even anger when their core positions are challenged.

> "We should be unafraid to doubt. There is no believing without some doubting, and believing is all the more robust for having experienced its doubts."
>
> **—JUSTIN HOLCOMB**

Exacerbating this situation is the fact that many of us get a majority of our news from social media, platforms that curate the information we receive based on our past behavior, stated preferences, and our peer set. This creates a strong propensity for confirmation bias as we are exposed to stories and opinions that support the views we already have—some of which are unsubstantiated rumors or outright lies (e.g., fake news). This is a very dangerous phenomenon that we all need to be more aware of.

While we need vision, conviction, and confidence to be successful, we also need to balance that with doubt, healthy skepticism, and humility.

Here are a few more benefits of having doubt and openly contemplating it with others:

- It keeps us open to new ideas and perspectives.
- It keeps us humble and motivated (overconfidence is often a precursor to failure).
- It causes us to question more and to test our own assumptions more carefully.

Four Benefits of Travel

Between family vacation and business travel, I was recently in three different countries over the past three weeks, which offered some unique perspectives. At Acceleration Partners, we talk a lot about getting out of our comfort zones (in a mental sense), but there is something to be said for physically getting out of your comfort zone through travel. I believe there are four important benefits to travel and the accompanying change of scenery:

1. **New perspectives:** When you get out of your regular environment, the conversations change, and the new surroundings stimulate fresh perspectives. When I travel with someone who is in a new place for the first time, I'm always amazed at how the conversation transitions from the usual day-to-day nuances to observations and perspectives about where we are, new experiences, the culture, etc.

2. **Getting off autopilot:** When our world gets small, we get comfortable doing and talking about the same things. Essentially, we run on autopilot. When you travel and your routine is disrupted, there are suddenly a lot of new challenges and opportunities to figure things out and gain confidence through trial and error. A great example of this is navigating public transportation systems in new cities.

> "The world is a book and those who do not travel read only one page."

—ANONYMOUS

3. **New ideas:** When you are in a new place, your mind is exposed to new things, and your cognitive function is more active with your autopilot disengaged, stimulating new ideas. For example, the key aha moment for the idea for one of my businesses, BrandCycle, actually came about during a dinner and subsequent cab ride in Chicago several years ago.

4. **Appreciation of culture:** Increasingly, we are all global citizens. Understanding the power of culture and its applicability in different areas is fascinating and can really expand our horizons personally and professionally. One of my favorite examples is how our British friends have turned the negative "waiting in line" into the much more dignified "queuing up."

Random Act of Kindness

I made a deal with my seven-year-old son. In exchange for heading home early from our Fourth of July festivities, he could have two dollars to play the infamous claw game in the hotel game room. I'm sure you've seen these. It's a machine where the objective is to use a joystick to maneuver the metal claw in order to try and pick up a prize.

I have tried hopelessly over the years to convey to my kids that this game is rigged against them, but it was a small price to pay to beat the holiday traffic.

Zach tried unsuccessfully four times to pick up a Boston Celtics mini basketball before depleting his funds. Standing nearby, however, was a boy (around ten) who had cracked the code and had a collection of items that he had grabbed from the claw machine.

I reminded Zach of the deal we had made, and we began to leave. As we walked out, this boy came over and handed Zach the Celtics ball. He had seen him struggle for it and used his own money to grab it for him.

I'll never forget the look on Zach's face as he thanked the boy profusely. Then, when we tried to repay the boy the fifty cents he had spent, he reluctantly took it but then promptly gave it to another child as we walked away.

> "Three things in human life are important. The first is to be kind. The second is to be kind. And the third is to be kind."

—HENRY JAMES

When we got into the car, Zach blurted out, "Oh my gosh, I can't believe how nice that boy was!"

It was an amazing moment to see the impact that an act of kindness has through the eyes of a child. Rachel and I took the opportunity to tell him that he should remember how that made him feel and try to do the same for others.

In our busy lives, sometimes it's the smallest acts that can make a huge difference. For Zach, an act that cost fifty cents made his day—and hopefully taught him a lifelong lesson about being kind and generous to others. My only regret was that I wasn't able to find the boy's parents and compliment them on the values they had imparted to him.

Justifying Our Contradictions

Having just suffered through the third 2016 U.S. presidential debate, I was interested to watch the very partisan post-debate analysis. This is where intelligent people who represent the entrenched sides of the political spectrum blindly defend their candidate, even in the face of clear contradictions, fact-checking, and often indefensible positions. Why can't they step back and make an objective analysis of what they just witnessed?

One of the main reasons is the concept of cognitive dissonance, a subject I have become fascinated by ever since reading a book called *Mistakes Were Made, But Not by Me* a few years ago. The technical definition of cognitive dissonance from psychology is "the mental stress or discomfort experienced by an individual who holds two or more contradictory beliefs, ideas, or values at the same time."

In more simple terms, our brains want to insulate us from making mistakes, so they allow us to rationally justify contradictions in our mind. So rather than learning from our mistakes, we tend to double down and get further entrenched in our position as a defense mechanism. A few examples from the book:

When district attorneys are presented with irrefutable DNA evidence that exonerates someone who they convicted years earlier, they double down (often coming out of retirement) to

> "He that complies against his will is of his own opinion still."

> **—SAMUEL BUTLER**

prove that the person is guilty. Why? Because they do not want to believe they could have put an innocent person in jail.

When followers of a cult are told the world is going to end on a certain day and that day passes with no fiery inferno, the leader of the cult usually picks a new date, and the followers double down. Why? Because they can't believe they would have fallen for a scam; ergo, it must be true.

Cognitive dissonance studies have also shown that our satisfaction level is much higher when we do something that was difficult to obtain/achieve because we are convincing ourselves that it had to be worth the effort. This has a lot of implications for businesses, social groups, fraternities, etc. It also contributes to our inability to cut our losses.

Recognizing cognitive dissonance in yourself helps to promote a growth mindset and ability to learn from mistakes. Recognizing it in others can be a powerful tool in negotiation as it often explains why someone might be acting irrationally or defensively. Remember that they may need a graceful, face-saving exit from their entrenched position.

What have you convinced yourself of that might not be true?

What Really Matters

The holidays are a favorite time of the year for many of us and for good reason. We have the opportunity to spend quality time with friends and family and take a step back to reflect on what and who matter most in our lives. Unfortunately, that feeling is often short-lived as we jump back into the new year and our routines.

If you believed you only had a few minutes to live, might it change your perspective or behavior more permanently? This is the story of Ric Elias, the founder of Red Ventures.

On January 15, 2009, Ric's flight (US Airways 1549) hit a flock of birds right after takeoff from New York and lost power in both engines. In his emotional five-minute TED Talk, Ric reflects on what went through his mind as the now famous Captain "Sully" Sullenberger prepared for an improbable crash landing on the Hudson River. Sully's only words to his passengers were, "brace for impact," leaving Ric and 154 other passengers to suddenly contemplate their mortality in what they believed were the last minutes of their lives.

Thankfully, everyone survived, and the event is now referred to as "the miracle on the Hudson".

Here are three things Ric took away from that day:

"As we express our gratitude, we must never forget that the highest appreciation is not to utter words but to live by them."

—JOHN F. KENNEDY

1. Everything changes in an instant. Don't wait for the "right moment."
2. Remove negative energy from your life. Resolve to be happy, not "right."
3. Recognize what is most important. For Ric, his most important goal in life was to be a good dad.

Problem Solving

After a recent trip to Spain, I realized how much technology aided my wife and me during our vacation. Easy and fast access to the internet via our smartphones made renting a car and finding our way around a new place a very different and less stressful experience than just ten years ago. Now, if you take a wrong turn, Google Maps puts you back on the right path in seconds. There are even apps that will translate a menu or webpage, and you can always look up feedback ratings for everything.

In contrast, when a friend and I took a backpacking trip around Europe over twenty years ago, we were armed only with traveler's checks, a *Let's Go Europe* book, a hostel card, and a Eurail Pass. We made our way through Europe with no real plan or easy way to communicate with home.

In many cities we visited, we arrived late at night without a place to stay. We had to sort our way through a new train system, city maps, and foreign languages just to find a suitable hostel with beds available—all things that would likely be performed today by an app.

None of our challenges were life-threatening, but they did require us to get out of our comfort zones, figure things out, and immerse ourselves in the local culture. In retrospect, the experience was invaluable.

> "The problem is not that there are problems. The problem is expecting otherwise and thinking that having problems is a problem."
>
> **—THEODORE ISAAC RUBIN**

I recently read through the journal that I kept during our journey, and it was eye-opening. As I read through my entries, I kept thinking, "What would my parents have thought if they knew these details?" I then realized that because they didn't/ couldn't know, we were both better off.

Reviewing my journal made me further appreciate that although technology has many benefits, it can also have its drawbacks. My daughter has realized this as well. During our trip, she sent us the opening of a speech she gave while at overnight camp titled, "Disconnecting to Connect." She spoke about the benefits of being offline for most of the summer, which gave her a chance to really connect with those around her.

What I've learned is that in the end, when we don't learn to solve little problems, we find ourselves getting derailed by speed bumps and unable to tackle bigger problems down the road. What's needed is a shift in our mindset to embrace the challenges before us and see problems as opportunities to learn, grow, connect, and interact with the world around us in new ways.

Embracing Relationships

Recently, I had dinner with someone I have worked with for years. While we've developed a strong working relationship, we hadn't had the opportunity to catch up socially. I really enjoyed learning more about their background and life outside work. It also reminded me why one of our company's core values is "Embrace relationships." Here's how we define this core value:

Relationships advance our personal and professional lives, contributing greatly to our successes. We focus on long-term outcomes, meaningful relationships, and genuine connections with our clients, teammates, and partners. We believe that competence and character are fundamental to relationships built on trust and that quality relationships allow us to achieve more.

As it turns out, in addition to being a guiding business principal, this core value may have the side benefit of helping us live longer.

In a 2017 *Inc.* article, "This 75 Year Harvard Study Found the 1 Secret to Living a Fulfilling Life," the author reviewed two contemporaneous Harvard studies (Grant and Glueck) that tracked the physical and emotional well-being of two populations over a period of seventy-five years. The Glueck Study looked at 456 men living in inner-city Boston neighborhoods between 1939 and 2014. The Grant Study looked at 268

|| "Everybody needs somebody."

— **MAHALIA JACKSON**

male Harvard graduates from the classes of 1939–1944. The lengthy time frame of the study required multiple generations of researchers who analyzed blood samples, conducted brain scans, and examined self-reported surveys and interaction to compile the findings.

What the consolidated study concluded is that when it comes to having a happy, healthy life, there is one thing that surpasses all the rest in terms of importance: good relationships. According to Robert Waldinger, director of the Harvard Study of Adult Development, "The clearest message that we get from this seventy-five-year study is this: Good relationships keep us happier and healthier. Period."

An important distinction the study made is that the quantity of friends had little to no impact on happiness; it was the quality of the relationship that mattered. And what drives the quality and depth of a relationship? The authenticity and vulnerability we bring to it. The studies' authors also stressed that when we hit the inevitable rough patches in our lives, it's critical to do everything we can to lean into these relationships and not push them away.

So the next time you're scrolling through your Facebook or

Instagram posts, liking things along the way, you might instead think about using that time to pick up the phone and connect with someone you care about. Likewise, in business, rather than seeing someone as just an employee, client, prospect, or customer, engage with them as a person. Doing so could develop into an important relationship and may even help you live longer.

Bad Week

A Sunday in April 1981 started off a very bad week for Dr. Mary-Claire King. Her husband declared that he was leaving on vacation the next day with one of his graduate students and, subsequently, leaving their marriage.

On Monday, King learned that she had made tenure, but the high of that good news was greatly diminished when she returned home to find her house had been burglarized.

That Friday, King was scheduled to fly to DC to give an important presentation to the National Institutes of Health to make a case for her first research grant.

King's mother had come to town to watch King's six-year-old daughter, Emily, while King was in DC. However, shortly after arriving, her mother accused King of being the reason her family was falling apart, saying things like, "How could you do this? How could you not put your family first?" She then decided to promptly return home.

At this point, King had no one to watch Emily. So she called her mentor and told him that she wasn't going to be able to make her trip to DC. He told King to bring her daughter with her to DC and that he'd sit with Emily while King gave her presentation. He even bought Emily a plane ticket.

In the end, King was able to give her presentation and get

> "Our greatest glory is not in never falling but in rising every time we fall."
>
> **—OLIVER GOLDSMITH**

the grant for her research project, which ultimately became the identification of BRCA1—one of the largest discoveries in breast cancer to date. King has been working on this research for over thirty-three years.

King's story has several important lessons and reminders.

- We all need a mentor(s) in our lives to push us forward in our darkest, most difficult times. Friends, while supportive, will often just give us the out if we ask for it.
- We all have bad days, weeks, and even months. The question is not whether they will happen but how we handle them. Can we laugh off our bad luck, or do we get immobilized by despair?
- It was Thomas Fuller who once noted that, "the darkest hour is just before the dawn." Just when you think it can't get any worse, it might, but then it's likely to get better quickly. What's most important is finding a way to keep moving forward.

Mary-Claire King had every reason to quit that week. Very

few would have blamed her for doing so. However, had she quit, it's likely that millions of women's lives would not have been saved by her groundbreaking research.

Conclusion:
What Did You Need?

What I've loved most about writing Friday Forward over the years and seeing it grow has been hearing from readers. Each week, someone writes to me to share how getting the right message at the right time made a huge difference for them. It's this outcome—making an impact on someone I've never met—that keeps me writing.

I also love hearing from readers who share Friday Forward with people in their companies, families, and book groups.

We rely on each other for many things in life—for inspiration, guidance, emotional support, and accountability. But it can be difficult for us to understand or express what exactly we need at various points in life.

I say this from my own experience. I have a passion for sharing these types of ideas with others—pushing limits, continuously learning, building a life oriented around purpose and values—because those exact lessons were what I needed at crucial points in my life. There have been many instances where I've felt unfulfilled or that my potential was being wasted.

This was the case as early as childhood, where many of the strengths that I rely on today were seen as weaknesses or distractions. My energy and occasional inability to focus often frustrated many of my teachers, and I still have the many early report cards to prove it.

After graduating college, I performed best when I had a strong mentor, I was engaged in my work, and could focus on my strengths. It wasn't until I leapt into entrepreneurship that I started on the path I am on today, and it was many more years before I put all the pieces together.

I've heard the phrase: "Great leaders don't create followers. They create more leaders." Though I didn't realize it at the beginning, this a key part of the vision for Friday Forward. It's crucial for each of us to give the people around us the inspiration and support they need to be their best.

To close, I want you to think of a time where you struggled, really struggled. It could be either a recent challenge you faced or something from as far back as childhood. As you read earlier, often our purpose in life comes from a point of pain, but many of us don't make the connection, even when it's staring us right in the face.

When you think back on that challenge, ask yourself: What

did you need at the time? What advice or mentorship could have helped you? What can you do now to be the person who gives that guidance or support to somebody else?

We all depend on one another at one time or another. What's perhaps most positive about capacity building is that when we build our capacity, we can inspire the people around us to do the same. As Robert Ingersoll said, we rise by lifting others.

Sadly, this is not happening enough in the world today, but it's what is needed most. It can start with the simplest of efforts. Maybe it's just a few words of encouragement or letting someone know their opinion matters. I never in a million years would have thought an email that I began writing to my team would reach so many people globally and have such an impact. But it also never would have happened if I not decided to just write that first note on a Friday in November.

We all have a responsibility to one another. What are you going to do to lift someone else up?

Acknowledgments

I have many people to thank who were part of my journey to writing this book. First and foremost, I want to thank the dedicated readers of Friday Forward (fridayfwd.com) who have shared my weekly messages with their teams, companies, and families and helped Friday Forward reach every continent in the world. It's your personal notes and messages that keep me writing each week.

To my incredible team at Acceleration Partners (AP), for their ongoing support of Friday Forward and for sharing the messages outside AP and making me realize they could have value beyond our own walls.

To Mick Sloan and Lenox Powell, for their weekly feedback and editing of my Friday Forwards. They help turn run-on sentences and typos into a clear and polished end product that makes a real impact.

To Brad, Ellie, JT, Tucker, and the Scribe Media team, for all their support and hard work in bringing this original concept to life.

To Rick Pascocello, for taking an interest in my writing and encouraging me to push forward.

To my agent, Richard Pine, for taking me on, and the entire Inkwell Management team for their support.

To my editor, Meg Gibbons, for her continued support for my writing and new ideas. Also to Dominique Raccah, Liz Kelsch, Morgan Vogt, Kavita Wright, Erin McClary, and the entire Sourcebooks team for their support and excitement for both *Elevate* and *Friday Forward*.

Last but never least, this book is dedicated to my wife, Rachel, and to my three children, Chloe, Max, and Zach. It is because of their love and support and their willingness to put up with me that I am able to focus on my writing and make the impact with my life that I know is possible.

About the Author

Robert Glazer is the founder and CEO of global partner marketing agency Acceleration Partners. A serial entrepreneur, Bob has a passion for helping individuals and organizations build their capacity to elevate.

Under his leadership, Acceleration Partners has received numerous industry and company culture awards, including Glassdoor's Employees' Choice Awards (two years in a row), *Ad Age*'s Best Place to Work, *Entrepreneur*'s Top Company Culture (two years in a row), Great Place to Work and *Fortune*'s Best Small and Medium Workplaces (three years in a row), and *Boston Globe*'s Top Workplaces (two years in a row). Bob was also named to Glassdoor's list of Top CEOs of Small and Medium Companies in the U.S. for two straight years, ranking as high as number two.

Bob's writing reaches over five million people around the globe each year who resonate with his topics, which range from performance marketing and entrepreneurship to company culture, capacity building, and leadership. Bob has been a columnist for *Forbes, Inc.,* Thrive Global, and *Entrepreneur* and has also had his articles published in *Harvard Business Review, Fast Company, Success Magazine,* and more. Worldwide, he is a sought-after speaker by companies and organizations on subjects related to business growth, culture, building capacity, and performance. He is the host of *The Elevate Podcast,* where he chats with CEOs, authors, thinkers, and top performers about the keys to achieving at a high level.

Bob also shares his ideas and leadership insights via Friday Forward, a popular weekly inspirational newsletter that reaches over two hundred thousand individuals and business leaders across over sixty countries.

He is the author of the *Wall Street Journal* and *USA Today* bestseller *Elevate* and the international bestselling book *Performance Partnerships.*

Outside work, Bob can likely be found skiing, cycling, reading, traveling, spending quality time with his family, or overseeing some sort of home renovation project.

Learn more about Bob at robertglazer.com.

Resources

For more information on capacity building, I encourage you read my other book, *Elevate: Push Beyond Your Limits and Unlock Success in Yourself and Others.*

I am always interested in new ideas, partnerships, and feedback and would love to hear from you. Feel free to drop a line at elevate@robertglazer.com. I work to read every email and respond to most.

Please leave a review:

If you enjoyed *Friday Forward*, I'd love to ask you to leave a rating and review on your favorite bookseller website. It's the best way to help other people discover the book, learn from the content, and help others.

robertglazer.com/review

Official Friday Forward book site:

robertglazer.com/forward

The Elevate Podcast

Hear in-depth conversations with the world's top CEOs, authors, thinkers, and performers, including many of the thought leaders mentioned in this book!

robertglazer.com/podcast

More about me:

To learn more about me, my writing or speaking, and partnerships opportunities, please visit

robertglazer.com

About my company:

accelerationpartners.com

ELEVATE

A *Wall Street Journal* and *USA Today* Bestseller from Robert Glazer

To learn more about how you can build capacity in your daily life and emulate the examples in *Friday Forward*, check out Robert Glazer's global bestselling book, *Elevate. Elevate: Push Beyond Your Limits and Unlock Success in Yourself* digs deeper into the four elements of capacity building outlined in *Friday Forward* and provides an actionable framework you can use to make lasting changes in your life. *Friday Forward* gives the motivation to improve, and *Elevate* provides a road map.

> "Bob Glazer is an unusually forward-thinking leader, and in this book he highlights some of his most inspiring lessons about how to bring out the best in yourself and others."
> —**Adam Grant**, *New York Times* **bestselling author of** *Give and Take* **and** *Originals*, **and host of the TED podcast** *WorkLife*

> "In an act of real generosity and vulnerability, Glazer shares his recipe for integrating spiritual, intellectual, physical, and emotional growth to build one's capacity. We can all learn from his example, his wisdom, and also the mistakes he's brave enough to share on the journey to elevate himself and countless others!"
> —**Kim Scott**, **author of** *Radical Candor: Be a Kickass Boss without Losing Your Humanity*

Learn more at **robertglazer.com/elevate**

FRIDAY FORWARD STORIES ONLINE

To find the online versions of the Friday Forward stories featured in this book for sharing and related content, please visit:

fridayfwd.com/stories

JOIN FRIDAY FORWARD

Also, if you haven't yet, sign up to receive Friday Forward each week by going to **robertglazer.com/join** or by scanning the QR code below.

HEAR MORE FROM THE LEADERS WHO INSPIRE FRIDAY FORWARD

I've been fortunate to have the chance to interview several of the people featured in this book on my podcast. Follow the QR codes below to hear my conversations with these transformational leaders and thinkers.

Philip McKernan, featured in Moment of Clarity (page 8):

Dandapani, featured in Energy Vampires (page 115):

Hal Elrod, featured in Early Riser (page 50):

Warren Rustand, featured in With Gratitude (page 118):

Eric Kapitulik, featured in Goals and Standards (page 71):

Conor Neill, featured in Having Doubt (page 128):

Sean Swarner, featured in Trough and Peak (page 83):